The Craftsman in Textiles

LESLIE J. CLARKE

The Craftsman in Textiles

FREDERICK A. PRAEGER, *Publishers*

New York · Washington

BOOKS THAT MATTER

Published in the United States of America in 1968
by Frederick A. Praeger, Inc., Publishers
111 Fourth Avenue, New York, N.Y. 10003

Library of Congress Catalog Card Number: 68-28338

Printed in Great Britain

TO MY WIFE

CONTENTS

THE PLATES

Between pages 64 and 65

Preface

THIS book is not a textbook for students of textile technology but is an attempt to tell in simple language the story of one of the most complicated of the useful arts which grew to its full flowering long before the ages of steam and electricity.

Like M. Jourdain who had been speaking prose long before he knew the word, man had perceived many problems for which he had worked out empirical solutions.

That these discoveries were happy accidents is too plausible an explanation to be acceptable; what is clear is that even before there were written records of his activities the inventive man with a speculative mind was an active member of society as was the artist seeking to express his ideas in concrete form. By a happy chance the two qualities existed side by side in the same person and it is in this sense that the word 'Craftsman' should be understood.

When in the 19th century the steam engine and the machine came in at the door, good taste flew out of the window, artists withdrew to their studios leaving manufacture to the 'rude mechanicals' and so the description—machine made—became synonymous with bad taste and poor quality.

Today we realise that this need never have happened and so all over the world design is being brought back as a subject of study; one worthy of being promoted by such organisations as the Design Centre and also important enough to be taught in schools and colleges.

The natural order of the world is chaos, metal forms lumps, and threads a tangled mass and it is only by great skill and ingenuity that man has imposed discipline and order, making material obedient to his purpose, and it is to tell the story of how this was done in the field of textiles that this book has been written, hoping that it will increase the pleasure of those who love beautiful and ingenious things by telling them what the weaver does and how he does it.

CHAPTER ONE

Warp and Weft

WHEN the curtain rises on the written story of man's history as a civilised being we discover that craftsmen, working in various materials, had already reached a high degree of skill; the Old Testament refers frequently to potters, carpenters, metalworkers and weavers, and the evidence of the archaeologist shows how many of the basic problems of technology were successfully solved by men whose names we shall never know and who left behind no written record, so that only by studying their works can we get insight into their skill, ingenuity and love of beauty.

These three qualities deserve a moment's study because they are the triple hall-marks of the true craftsman, to whom the question, 'What is it for?' is perfectly sensible—a chair must be strong enough to bear weight, and comfortable to sit in, and if ornamentation interferes with these basic qualities then the carpenter has laboured in vain.

Just as the grain of wood is both its beauty and weakness, so each textile material and fabric has opposite qualities which can only be reconciled by skill and ingenuity; but the craftsman, being by nature also an artist, seeks not only to overcome these difficulties but at the same time to express in colour, form and texture abstract ideas which will give pleasure both to himself as a creative artist, and to the beholder. It is in resolving this conflict between beauty and utility that the craftsman finds his keenest pleasure.

While it is obvious that a chair must be useful it may not be so clear that the products of the weaver's art must also be tested by similar standards. At a first glance nothing could appear more frivolous and carefree than a little girl's hair ribbon, but if we stop to think we shall realise that apart from being a pretty ornament it must comply with a strict specification. It must be thin in texture so as to make a small knot, nevertheless it must be crisp and firm so that the ends of the bow stand out bravely; because bows tend to come undone or to slip off the hair it must have a surface which is not slippery and, because the tying of a bow ends in a vigorous tug, it must have good tensile strength. No decorative design, however charming, must interfere with these basic qualities. In a later chapter we shall see how this dilemma is resolved and why out of the multitude of fabrics which might be used only one—taffeta—satisfies these requirements and how within this framework, the weaver can in a variety of ways add decorative effects.

When Johnny went to the fair to buy 'A pretty blue ribbon to tie up my bonny brown hair' he little thought that behind his love token would lie a little masterpiece of the weaver's art.

The story of the weaver can be divided into three main chapters; the first will tell of what men did and how they did it in that great outburst of technical inventiveness which we speak of as the Stone, Bronze and Iron ages. The second will tell of the part played by the weaver in the industrial revolution of the 18th and 19th centuries when the application of machines to manufacture increased man's ability to produce an abundance of things by divorcing the hitherto inseparably linked words 'labour and laborious'. It was in textiles that, by a happy alliance with his brother craftsmen, the woodworker and the metal worker, the weaver blazed the trail which led to the modern industrial age.

Thirdly we shall see that when the chemist and the physicist broke through to the second industrial revolution by their discoveries that man was not necessarily dependent on nature for his raw materials, but could evolve new and exciting substances, hitherto undreamed of, it was the weaver who by adapting and improving his ancient craft skill helped to make nylon a household word.

Dr. Johnson defined weaving as: 'An art by which threads of any substances are crossed and interlaced so as to be arranged into a perfectly expanded form, and thus be adapted for covering other bodies.'

Two hundred years after they were written the Doctor's words still deal with the subject with admirable clarity and brevity; and except to add that in the modern world textiles have other and more exciting uses than 'The covering of other bodies', we can scarcely do better than expand his text by a series of chapters explaining how and why the substances are selected and how they are interlaced.   Whether we study the most primitive hand loom or the most modern fully automatic loom we can define them as machines for the interlacing of threads.   It is by his control of this interlacing that the weaver achieves two objectives, rigidity or strength and surface texture which will be pleasing both to the eye and to the touch.

However complex a fabric may appear to be there are two simple basic elements into which it can be analysed:

Warp: Which consists of a number of strong smooth threads laid parallel to one another and stretching from end to end of the piece of cloth.   They are kept under tension, and form the foundation of the fabric.

Weft: Usually softer and more pliable threads passing backwards and forwards from side to side.   Weft may serve two purposes: (*a*) to bind the warp into a web, or (*b*) to weave in a more free manner so as to create ornamental effects.

Warp and weft therefore intersect at right angles, and so if we have a 100 warp threads per inch woven with 50 weft threads per inch we shall have 5,000 intersections per square inch.   If this number seems at first sight surprising it should be pointed out that a pocket handkerchief has a count of 80 × 80, i.e. 6,400 intersections per square inch.

Large as these numbers may be, nevertheless at each intersection only one of two things can happen—the warp thread can pass over the weft or the weft can pass over the warp (Figure 1).

Therefore, however great may be the number of intersections only two choices are possible; and out of these basic elements all woven fabrics are constructed. We are all aware that out of the limited notes of the musical octave repeated at various pitch levels and by varying voice or instrument tones a great work such as Bach's B Minor Mass is built, but it may come as a surprise to learn that one of the largest pieces of fabric in the world, the great tapestry hanging in Coventry Cathedral is, notwithstanding its complexity of colour and design, built up out of these two simple elements A and B (Figure 1).

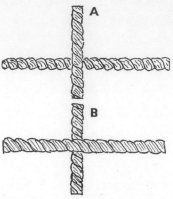

Figure 1. The fundamental weave

This apparent paradox calls for a little further study because at first sight it might appear that if we have 6,400 intersections per square inch, each of which can be either A or B, then astronomical numbers of fabrics could be evolved by exploring all the permutations and combinations which the mathematician would tell us are possible; but just as Bach was limited by the laws of harmony, and the physical limits of each voice or instrument to a restricted selection, so is the weaver bound by the fundamental rules of fabric structure to a surprisingly small number of combinations; and, just as many musical intervals are either unpleasant discords or unsingable, so would many fabrics possible in theory fail to satisfy Dr. Johnson's definition of 'perfectly expanded form'.

When we consider the variety of musical compositions and woven fabrics we begin to see that a good definition of a master craftsman is 'one who, working within the restrictions imposed by his resources nevertheless achieves the maximum freedom of artistic expression'.

We must now study in more detail these basic rules of fabric structure which govern the weaver and, by a curious coincidence, the eight notes of the musical octave are matched by the same number of warp and weft threads out of which the great fundamental weaves are created. In a later chapter we shall see how this limitation was overcome, but that was a long way along the road which starts with primitive man making his first efforts in fabric geometry; but for the moment let us be content to study this octave and see what harmonies were produced from it. For this purpose we need a system of notation and squared paper serves very well. If we take a piece of graph paper and let each vertical row of squares represent a warp thread and each horizontal row a weft thread then each square represents an intersection. By painting in or leaving blank we can therefore show whether at any particular point warp is over weft or vice versa; such diagrams are known as drafts and several are shown in Figure 2.

When the shuttle of a loom makes its journey from one side of the warp to the other we say it has made a pick and by our squared paper we can record how each pick of weft behaves as it crosses successive warp threads. How this is achieved is another story and in a later chapter we shall study the mechanics of the loom, but for the moment let us think of warp and weft floating in space.

THE FOUR GREAT BASIC WEAVES

Out of the great number of weaves possible on eight warp and eight weft threads there are four which experience has shown to be of practical value, and most of the fabric ever produced is based on one of these, either directly or by some modification. By suitable selection of the nature and thickness of the threads great variety of cloths may be produced, for example the finest lawn or crêpe-de-chine is exactly the same weave as hessian or potato sacking, the first being woven from the finest cotton, the second from real silk and the last from jute; in each case however the weave is the same:

B

Ground or Tabby

This is the simplest of all weaves and was no doubt the first to be invented. In order to make it, all we have to do is to pass the weft across the warp twice: the first time causing it to pass over all the odd warp threads and under the the evens while on the second passage we go over the evens and under the odds (Figure 2A).

The points to notice about this weave are:

(*a*) Both faces of the cloth are identical.
(*b*) It gives the firmest interlocking of warp and weft.
(*c*) Unless the threads are exceptionally coarse it has a matt surface free from any grain.
(*d*) If the warp and weft are of different colours we get a perfect 50/50 blend because the individual intersections are so small that black and white blend into grey so far as the eye is concerned.

Figure 2B shows a modification in which each pick is duplicated; this makes a heavy rib and is called grogram, and this, if broken into blocks makes a basket weave or Barathea (Figure 2C).

Plain Twills

All twills have one characteristic in common, they show a pronounced diagonal trail caused by moving the starting point of a weave sequence one place to right or left on each successive pick. Suppose we decide to use an over three and under one arrangement, then by moving our starting-point one thread to the right we get the result shown in Figure 2D.

The characteristic features of this weave are:

(*a*) Having less intersections than the ground weave the cloth is softer and more flexible.
(*b*) Except for the 2 and 2 sequence the two faces will be different, the one predominantly weft and the other warp.
(*c*) If warp and weft are of different colours this will cause pronounced diagonal coloured stripes.

Fancy Twills

If we go on weaving a twill as above the trailing lines join up and give the impression that they start at one edge of the fabric and run out at the opposite side, but we can reverse the direction if we wish by changing our starting point from the order 1, 2, 3, 4, to 4, 3, 2, 1 and by so doing make herring-bone patterns.

By making the reversal after some number of picks, our herring-bone will have points in the direction of the weft, but by reversing after so many warp ends we shall get herring-bone with points in the direction of the warp (Figure 2E). Here the weave itself is creating a pattern, the zigzag line found on ancient pottery and used by the Normans in their stone arches.

If we combine our two herring-bone weaves we have produced a diamond pattern (Figure 2F). The thing to note about this is that we did not think of zigzags or diamonds, we experimented on our loom by changing the sequence of weaving and so created a little design for which we then thought of a name after creating it; then we put it on paper for record purposes.

This is a point about weaving which we must note carefully, the weaver has an idea, tries it out and gets a design—the loom is a creative instrument played on by a creative artist.

Satins

So far we have cautiously moved one step at a time forwards or sideways, but what happens if we make less regular jumps? Suppose we move one step forward and skip over two threads between our intersections (Figure 2G). This is, of course, a 7 and 1 twill broken up and on paper looks rather unpromising, but because threads are really long slender cylinders they therefore have highlights running along them, the position of which will change according to the angle at which the light is reflected. When we try this out on the loom the effect is delightful. The fabric will be discovered to be soft and rich in appearance with a beautiful sheen. If our warp threads are closely packed they will lose their individuality and merge together into a perfectly smooth surface without grain but having a polished surface. The softness

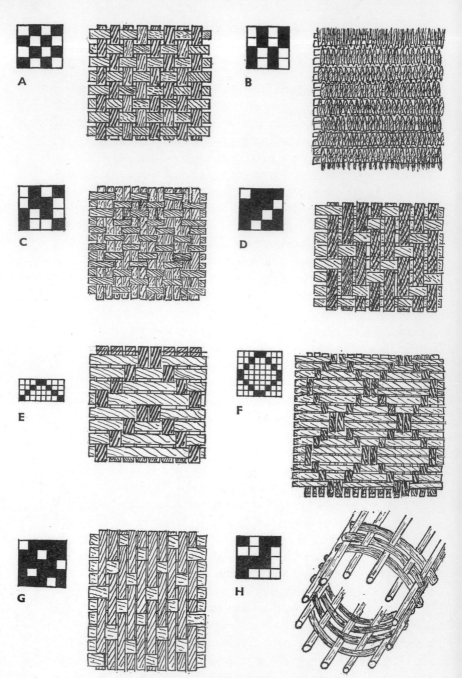

Figure 2. Eight different fabric structures

of the fabric will cause it to drape into rounded folds and these, reflecting the light at different angles, will give a richness of effect beyond anything we have produced so far. In calling it a satin we have added a new word to the dictionary, i.e. 'Satin, adjective = sumptuous and lustrous'.

Clearly the question arises—Why limit ourselves to eight thread repeats of our patterns? If we go beyond this number our cloth will grow weaker and flabbier, in fact it may even break into holes because the intersections are too scattered.

Tubular Fabrics

There are a number of end uses which call for fabric to be woven in the form of a seamless tube; for example, fire hose, pillow cases, underwear shoulder straps and filter tubes.

The actual weave employed is usually one of the simple basic ones but many people would assume that some form of rotary machine should be employed; in fact, by an ingenious trick of the trade, an ordinary loom whose shuttle goes backwards and forwards in a straight line is all that is required, provided the warp is manipulated in the correct way, which is as follows:

Although, as already stated, a ground or taffeta only requires two warp ends and picks when woven as a single cloth, in tubular form we must have duplicate warp ends and each pick must be made twice so as to weave on alternate faces of the cloth. Because only one continuous weft is used, the two fabrics will be bound together at the edges, but the warp is selected in a special way so that the odd numbered threads weave the upper face and the even ones the lower face; when the shuttle is making the lower face all the odd warps must be lifted up out of the way and one of the two evens, and thus four warp ends and four picks make a repeat of the pattern.

Figure 2H shows the draft of this and an isometric view of the fabric; this is, for sake of clearness, shown in circular form but in practice it comes out of the loom as a flattened tube; which, if it is needed in circular form, must be set by subsequent heat treatment.

There is one special application of tubular weave where

aesthetic considerations are its justification and that is ribbon weaving.   In broad fabric the selvedges are cut off and discarded, but in ribbons the edge must be both smooth and ornamental and the only way to ensure this is to have a small independent warp on either side and to allow this to make a fine tube.   Although small, this edge warp is very rich and the weft is completely concealed. The ribbons used on mens' felt or bowler hats are good examples of this use of tubular weave.

CHAPTER TWO

Ornament and Design

ANYONE who visits a museum or studies the illustrations in a book on archaeology must be struck by the fact that no sooner had man discovered how to shape stone, clay or metal into objects, than he began to apply decoration, at first by little more than scratched lines, but soon growing into elaborate patterns. When we think how great must have been the labour of making even the simplest thing, it would at first sight appear that the worker would stop as soon as he had produced a plain utility article; but he did not; he went on to lavish further care on his product, clearly driven by some powerful motive.

As human nature does not change over the ages we have no need to speculate about this question because there are today craftsmen at work and we can study what they do and why they do it. The first thing to realise is that the true craftsman is a creative artist with a strong sense of individuality which he seeks to express by his designs, and at the same time he is a man who revels in the battle between himself and the reluctance of his material to assume the form he desires. Nothing illustrates this better than the story of our great cathedrals, where we learn that sometimes the tower fell down or the walls collapsed because the mason's technical resources were inadequate for the ambitious and noble themes his imagination had conceived.

But there is another side to the story:—craftsmen feel no sense of shame in admitting that they make things for other people in return for money, and the reaction of the customer is a powerful influence on the designer, only Robinson Crusoe could please himself as to what he made; and so the designer is under pressure to please his patron by appealing to his sense of individuality expressed by his taste.

If this were a book on the history of fashion we might indulge in fascinating discussion on why customers' taste moves in waves which, by their own growing impetus and weight, inevitably break and fall. The Victorian overmantel eventually collapsed by its own elaboration and the sheer weight of Goss china and bric-à-brac it had to support; but suffice it for us to note that the effect of fashion on the craftsman is to drive him to explore new techniques; Whittle was stimulated to design the jet engine because the piston engine had reached a point beyond which it could not develop to cope with the tasks it was called on to perform. The history of invention abounds in examples of devices which were evolved in response to consumer demand.

Textiles follow the same pattern, and we shall see that although the decorative possibilities of the simple weaves we have so far studied were very great, nevertheless there was a definite point beyond which the weave could not go unless a revolutionary idea in fabric construction could be thought of.

The Egyptians and the Peruvians

Fortunately for us we do not have to speculate on how the earliest weavers carried out their tasks, because the archaeologists can provide us with vivid pictures which early people made showing how things were done. Plate 4 shows a complete textile factory as it existed in Peru in 2500 B.C. So clear is the detail that we can see not only exactly how the loom was made and operated but how many colours were employed in the design. Hanging on the wall against each weaver is a sketch of the design on which each was working; and, just to give a homely touch, two people are serving drinks to the workers. The works canteen and the tea break have a more ancient history than perhaps we suspect.

In the case of the Egyptian weaving, the loom was very primitive consisting of a rectangular wooden frame on which the warp threads were stretched like the strings of a harp while the weft was inserted by hand; in fact the process was more like darning than weaving.

The Peruvian drawing is interesting because the artist with a fine eye for realism shows us not only how the loom was made, but also the patterns being woven.

Here the warp is stretched from a branch of a tree or a hook in the wall to a belt passing round the worker's waist so that he has control of the tension.   This back strap loom was in use all over the world among primitive peoples until modern times.

The important thing to note is that the actual weaving was done with the weaver's fingers which were used to interlace the weft threads, wound on small slender bobbins, among the warp threads. There is no evidence of any mechanical device for selecting warp threads and so it was by his own dexterity that the weaver controlled the interlacing of the threads in the order called for by the cloth.

It will also be noticed that the warp was of a fixed length so that each individual piece of fabric would be woven separately and probably for practical reasons did not exceed six feet in length.

The rainless climate of Peru has fortunately preserved for us a few specimens of this type of weaving, and so we can discern that cotton was the raw material and that already a range of vegetable dyes had been discovered.

The Chimu and Mochica Indians who wove these fine textiles were also brilliant potters who made life-like reproductions of the people and their activities and the clothes they wore.   A popular garment was a poncho or type of smock woven in check designs notable for the vigour and boldness of their treatment.

It is interesting to note that this Peruvian back strap weaving is still practised today for a special purpose.   Sick people who may be confined to bed for long periods suffer much from boredom, and it has been found that various handicrafts are a great aid to recovery.   As machinery cannot be used in bed the warp is tied to the rail at the foot of the bed and the other end to a belt round the patient's waist.   His fingers provide all else that is needed.

Few patients who benefit from this new remedial therapy realise that they are practising an art which was developed half-way round the world over 4,000 years ago.

First Steps In Pattern Making

So great is the diversity of patterns which became possible when the weaver's art, and with it the fully developed loom, were available that it will be simpler if we stop for a while and study what decorative effects were possible from the simple basic weaves we have so far mentioned.

As this is a chapter on weaving we are not here concerned with embroidery or dyeing, both of which are after processes, normally carried out on plain cloth.

The first and simplest patterns would be created when the weaver used several wefts, each of a different colour, and by this means produced stripes running from edge to edge of the cloth. As the weft was put in by hand there was no limit to the number of colours nor to the complexity of the stripe pattern. Even today this device is used in industry for the making of fancy striped club ties and blazer cloths. Using a plain black warp and a series of multi-coloured wefts, which can easily be changed, a wide range of patterns can easily be produced.

The next step was to make a multi-coloured warp laying so many threads of each colour, and by this means making any combination of widths and colour of stripe—a modern example being the well-known Macclesfield stripe fabrics. As an art form, however, warp stripes are of very limited value because all the patterns have a family likeness, sadly reminiscent of deck-chair canvas.

If, however, we combine weft stripes and warp stripes, i.e. we weave first a black and then a white weft on a black and white striped warp we get a new effect—the check pattern. If the change is made over a small number of threads, say two white and two black all across the warp, and make the weft changes of a similar frequency, the check is not obvious to the naked eye, but becomes a sort of granite texture especially if the weave chosen is the simple 2×2 twill. The majority of the cloths for mens' suitings are still made in this way, and great ingenuity is displayed in blending the colours.

The most elaborate and interesting cloth evolved from this simple combination of two stripes is the Highland tartan. Tartans are made from a warp having broad stripes of dark colours such as bottle green, navy blue or black with narrower stripes of bright colours such as red, gold or white. The weft colours are exactly the same and are inserted in a sequence which exactly matches the pattern of the warp. The result is a pattern

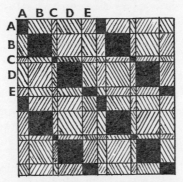

Figure 3. The construction of a tartan

of great complexity because as each weft thread crosses from side to side it interweaves with all the colours in succession. The result is that when it blends with its own colour we get a square of pure tone, i.e. white warp and white weft give a square of pure white, but with all other colours it forms a mixture, i.e. black-white, green-white, etc., and as the weave is a twill the effect is as though an artist had shaded a drawing by diagonal lines alternating in colour. Figure 3 shows how this happens and explains how one of the most complex patterns is evolved from three basic ideas. It is interesting to note that this type of ornamentation is also ideal for the end purpose of the cloth. A kilt calls for great skill in the tailoring and the cloth must be both dense and supple if the garment is to be warm and yet hang in the correct manner. Fine wool for warmth and twill weave for flexibility, and interlacing stripes for rich ornamental effects are all perfectly combined in a tartan.

By changing the material from wool to fine cotton or rayon and using pastel shades the popular dress fabrics known as ginghams, still one of the most popular types, are produced. These are woven on automatic power looms, but they are only doing more speedily what the earliest weavers created.

All these three pattern-making methods suffer from two serious drawbacks, they repeat themselves throughout the length and breadth of the cloth and also they are geometrical in form and we know that geometrical designs tend to become monotonous. The problem for the weaver therefore was to invent a method which would give freedom to introduce form and colour in a random manner, the choice being governed only by artistic fancy and taste. This must have been a formidable problem and yet, if we turn back to the Peruvian picture, we see that it was successfully solved; in fact each weaver in the picture is weaving a different pattern. All employed the same beautifully simple idea which is not dependent on any elaborate mechanical invention. All we have to do is to take a plain warp and two or three coloured shuttles which we use in a novel manner. All patterns so far involve the weft going from edge to edge of the cloth, but suppose we go so far across with the first weft, then continue a little farther with the second and then change to the third, on the second pick we throw each shuttle back to its starting point. Two problems still have to be solved, the cloth must be of such a construction that weft is dominant on the face of the cloth and where the change of colour takes place we have a joint to deal with—if these can be overcome we have invented one of the most versatile instruments of decoration known to man. We can now think of colour in terms of shape and form and, provided we have a multiplicity of shuttles, there is virtually no limit to the patterning resources at our command; we have in fact discovered:

Tapestry Weaving

Where and when and by whom this was originally discovered we do not know, but all over the world the same basic idea has been used since the earliest times. Ponchos in Peru and Mexico, rugs in Turkestan and Persia and wall hangings in Italy and France, all are applications of this weave.

For this fabric we need a fine strong warp under heavy tension and having relatively few ends per inch. The loom used is of the simplest kind and consists of an overhead beam from which the warp hangs vertically and the tension is usually produced by grouping the warp ends into bunches, each of which is tied to a weight. The dexterity of the weaver's fingers provides the mechanism. Soft, thick weft is always used in order to give solidity of colour. The actual weave is always a simple one,

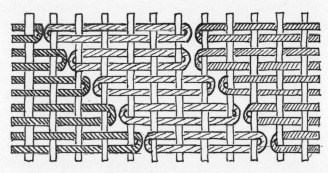

Figure 4. Tapestry weave

ground, i.e. odd and even interlacing, or the weft may pass over two or three and under the same number, returning in the reverse order, or in some cases the 3 and 1 twill weave is chosen. In certain oriental rugs the weft passes over three warp ends and is then actually wrapped completely round the fourth, moving one thread sideways on each successive pick.

Whichever modification of the weave is chosen, the effect so far as the eye is concerned is the same, a solid block of colour is produced. Figure 4 shows an enlarged view of a small unit of design woven in this way, and however complex the total design may be the method is the same. It is important to note that when a weft has finished a patch of colour it is cut off at the back, from which side the weaving is done, the design being observed through a mirror. The Lady of Shalott who saw the world in a mirror was clearly at her tapestry loom and Penelope who played for time by unpicking at night what she had woven by day was also a tapestry weaver.

In England tapestry maps of the counties of Salop, Hereford and Worcester were woven in Warwickshire under the direction of William Sheldon of Weston House about the year 1510, and these are today in the Bodleian Library at Oxford. In France in 1667 two brothers Giles and John Gobelin founded what became the most famous tapestry factory in the world. In recent times the tapestry which has become famous all over the world is that which forms the decoration covering the whole of the east wall of Coventry Cathedral. In fineness of detail and richness of colour it truly deserves the term 'Masterpiece'. Pessimists who enjoy such statements, 'There is no place for the craftsman in the modern world' might profitably visit Coventry Cathedral, where apart from the splendour of the architecture they will discover a treasure house of 20th-century craftsmanship in wood, iron, glass and textiles each example of which can stand comparison with the finest specimens of former ages.

When the design is formal or heraldic in character the weft is used in solid blocks of colour, but the fact that infinite changes of weft are possible enables the weaver, when the subject is pictorial, to imitate the gradation of tone similar to that used by the painter. This he does in two ways, either he has the threads dyed in the same dye both for longer and longer periods of time, thus producing a range of tones identical in hue but deeper and deeper in tone, or he uses multiple strands of weft of blended colours. The result is, so far as the eye is concerned, a heather mixture of great luminosity; for example magenta and bright green blend into a beautiful series of greys which are exceptionally clear and harmonise with all other colours. Some painters use this device and if we examine one of their paintings and a tapestry under a magnifying glass we shall see the affinity between the two methods.

The fact that the colour resources of the tapestry weaver are equal to those of the oil painter and that the tapestry loom is non-mechanical and so can be built of any size, gave a scope to design which was exploited for the production of wall coverings in the palaces of kings, and tapestry weaving often enjoyed royal patronage. The subject is a fascinating one and merits a volume to itself; those who want further information should read the article on Tapestry in the *Encyclopaedia Britannica* which has a series of excellent pictures both in black and white and in colour.

Pile Weaving

So far we have studied the resources available to the weaver from the interlacing of warp and weft, but a further development became possible when it was discovered how to introduce another set of threads standing up at right angles to the face of the cloth forming what is called pile. Velvets for dresses, Persian rugs and Wilton carpets are three examples of this type of weaving. In a later chapter we shall study the mechanisms by which this became possible on machinery, but at this stage it will be enough if we consider the principle on which these fabrics are constructed and try to understand wherein lies the beauty of this advanced form of weaving.

Since the ends of the pile are cut off they must be firmly anchored into a base fabric which provides the necessary strength and rigidity. This base fabric is nearly always the ground or 1 and 1 weave described on page 18. As mechanical efficiency is the only quality needed by this fabric the threads are fine and highly twisted; the pile threads being purely decorative are made from soft bulky yarn. All pile fabrics have two qualities in common, exceptional depth of tone of all colours, relieved by glowing highlights, so lustrous that even a black velvet will display silvery tones so that, when made into a garment, each movement of the wearer causes these reflections to move in a most pleasing way. Even perfectly plain velvet has a sumptuous look unequalled by any other fabric. The depth of tone is due to the shadows which form near the roots of the pile threads. Figure 5 shows a section of a pile fabric from which it will be seen that while the tips of the pile threads will be strongly illuminated we shall get progressively deeper shadows as we approach the base fabric. As the pile threads are never exactly at right angles to the base cloth the degree of illumination will vary according

Figure 5. Pile fabric

to the angle at which the light falls and from which the observer is looking. Anyone who has ever enjoyed the play of light and shade which we see when a breeze blows over a field of ripe corn will have seen an excellent illustration of this effect. A cornfield is a beautiful example of a pile fabric enormously magnified. Pile fabrics classified as velvets really involve the mechanism of a loom and will be dealt with in a later chapter, but carpets and rugs can be made by hand using a modification of the tapestry technique.

The tufting threads are cut into short lengths of about two inches and are inserted and knotted round a pair of warp threads by one of two types of knot—the Ghiordes or the Sehna. After each row of knots has been tied in, either one or two picks of plain weft are inserted right across the loom, so locking the knots in position and forming with the warp a firm base or back to the rug. The number of knots per square inch determines the quality of the carpet and may be as high as 400; as each end is tied in by the weaver's fingers it will be understood why good quality oriental rugs are luxury goods. The independence of the pile threads from the general fabric structure gives the weaver wide scope for pattern making.

The Effect of Light on Fabric

We tend to think of fabric as having length and width but ignore thickness except as a factor affecting warmth. Because threads are cylindrical, and are bent as they pass from one face of the cloth to the other, they have highlights and shadows.

The form and distribution of the highlights determines the luminosity of the surface and modifies the colour.

The attached diagrams, Figure 6, show two extremes of this effect. As a fine quality taffeta may have as many as 10,000 intersections of warp and weft per square inch, the eye sees a frosty sparkle, whereas in the satin the highlights are long and straight, like those seen on a polished knitting needle.

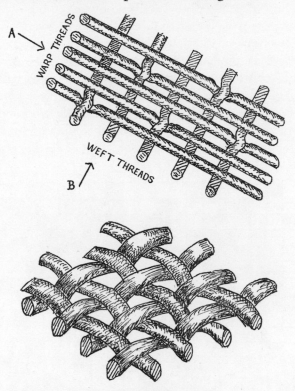

Figure 6. Satin (above) and taffeta

Rich satins may have 300 warp ends per inch, and the total effect is therefore like that of a polished flat surface.

The contrast between the brilliancy of a satin viewed along the warp and the dullness when viewed across it, is the explanation of two tones in a damask cloth, even though warp and weft are both the same colour.

By the delicate setting of the motions of the loom, and by varying the tension, the weaver has power to control or modify

c

these optical effects; and one of the marks of a master weaver is to make intelligent use of this property.

Damask

This fabric, which gets its name from the city of Damascus, is really a form of satin weave described on page 19 but so arranged that some parts have the warp face and some the weft face showing. If two squares of satin cloth are cut from the same piece and laid side by side, one being face up and the other face down, then in accordance with the explanation given above one will appear light and one dark, but if the observer shifts his viewpoint from a North–South axis to an East–West one, then the pieces will show the reverse effect, the dark one will be light and the light one dark. Figure 7 shows the treatment of a small unit of design arranged to

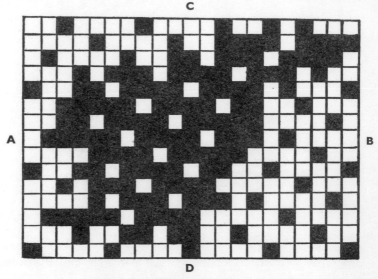

Figure 7. Damask pattern based on sleish satin

make use of this effect. The leaf is woven with satin warp face up and the surround with satin weft face up.

An observer looking along the line A–B will therefore see a glossy pale leaf on a dark ground, but if he shifts his position to the line C–D he will see a dark leaf on a pale ground. When one examines a white damask table cloth this effect is so strong that it is hard to believe that all the threads are white and that what seem to be contrasting areas of white and silver grey are optical illusions.

Fabrics woven in this way always have a sumptuous appearance and the damask weave produces magnificent curtains and furnishing fabrics.

A curtain hanging in folds will display every permutation and combination of tonal effects according to the angle at which the light falls.

How all this is achieved by the weaver must be left unexplained for the moment, but when we come to study the evolution of the loom we shall see in the Jacquard machine a triumph of ingenuity which made damask weaving easy.

Crêpes

It is hard to realise that the vast number of fabrics which go under this name are modifications of our simplest basic weave, the one and one ground, or such simple twills as two and two, or that the infinite variety of effects is due to light reflection while the delightful feel of such cloths, at once firm but supple, full but light, is due

Figure 8. Crêpe twist

to thread preparation—not to any weave device. A very simple experiment will suffice to show what is meant. Take a piece of string and stretch it between the two thumbs and fingers and then proceed by a rolling action to twist it more and more tightly. As long as the thread is kept under tension nothing will appear to have happened, but if we slightly relax the tension, first the thread will writhe into curves and may even run up into little tight loops like the letter s (Figure 8). This, suitably controlled, is the basis of all crêpes.   What happens is that when the cloth is woven the tension in the loom keeps the threads straight, and the cloth looks like ordinary taffeta, but on being allowed to relax the strain on the threads causes them to distort and twist into corkscrew curves. At the same time, instead of packing closely together the threads try to spring apart, giving a high degree of air space between the warp and weft threads.   It is the combination of light reflection from corkscrew curves explained on page 33 with bulky lightness which gives the crêpe weave its charm.   Regardless of changes in fashion crêpe in some form or other is always in demand.

The original and true crêpe is 'Crêpe-de-chine' woven from pure silk and having two wefts woven alternately, the first being twisted clockwise and the other anti-clockwise.   That is all. Discovered by some unknown Chinese genius it remains one of the great fabrics of the world.

If the weaver uses the technique of warp and weft patterning described on page 27 in association with crêpe technique the lines of the pattern become broken and distorted, but so fine is the grain that a delightful blend of colours is produced and this, coupled with the complex light reflection which we get from sinuous threads, explains why crêpe, which at first sight might be described as a plain fabric, is in fact full of life and sparkle.

Brocade Weaving

It was pointed out at the beginning of this chapter that unless warp and weft are interlocked at frequent intervals the fabric would become loose and unstable and therefore could not be used as cloth, in other words technical requirements put a limit to decorative effects.   Once this problem could be overcome the decorative possibilities open to the weaver would be greatly increased.

This was eventually achieved by using two or more shuttles weaving in quite different ways, the first one would carry a fine weft, usually matching the warp in colour and on its passage across the loom would interweave in one or other of the basic orders such as ground, twill or satin, so producing a firm plain cloth. The other shuttles could then be loaded with any other colour or type of yarn the weaver's fancy might require. When these went across the loom they could interweave in a free style which was purely decorative. Long floats were possible and, if so desired, the figuring weft could float across the back of the cloth, being brought on to the face only when required by the pattern.

Figure 9 shows how this method of weaving is applied to a

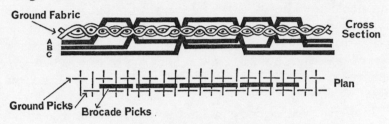

Figure 9. Brocade weaving

small section of a design worked in three brocade colours A, B and C on a taffeta ground whose warp and weft interweave in a 1 and 1 sequence, whereas the brocade wefts float either on the face or back according to the needs of the design. When a brocade weft floats on the face over more than twelve threads a tacking stitch or binder is used, but this is not visible to the naked eye. The pattern is therefore built up of a multiplicity of fine strips, but as the threads are in practice less than 1/100th of an inch in diameter, the eye sees only a solid mass; and because they are so small the square steps which form the outline of the design appear as a continuous curve. Many Macclesfield silk ties are woven in this way, and if they are examined under a magnifying glass the pattern will be seen to be built up in this way, and, if turned inside out, will show how the brocade wefts float on the back of the fabric. For the sake of tidiness these are usually bound by a tacking stitch formed by every 24 or 36 warp threads (these are not shown in the diagram), but these stitches are so minute that they are not visible to the naked eye, and also the fine floating design threads close up and conceal them.

Apart from tie silks mentioned above, the most common

examples of brocade weaving are curtain hangings and upholstery fabrics, and magnificent specimens of this type of work can be studied by visiting 17th- and 18th-century houses which are open to the public.

Archaeologists have now shown that as early as 6500 B.C. at Catal Huyuk men were weaving wool cloth which might be mistaken for a modern tweed suiting. While at Irgenhausen in Switzerland a linen cloth has been discovered woven in a delightfully bold brocade pattern. Solid masses of colour are contrasted with stripes and cross bars of two dice patterns, one fine and the other coarse. Both specimens belong to the neolithic age, which means that when Stonehenge was built the weaver had already evolved the basic weaves that are still used in the most modern weaving factories.

In this chapter the emphasis has been on what the weaver did and not how he did it, and there is no doubt that the basic fabric structures we have studied could all be produced by means of a frame on which warp could be tightly stretched, the rest being the result of nothing more than dextrous fingers; but in the next chapter we shall study how by mechanical ingenuity the loom was evolved as a wonderful and flexible instrument for the speedy and easy production of fabrics both useful and decorative.

CHAPTER THREE

The Weaver's Tools

ANYONE who wishes to practice the art of weaving as it was done in the earliest times may do so by taking a small picture frame and, after hammering in a row of panel pins along the top and bottom rails, make a warp by passing a ball of thread up and down, lapping it round a pin at each turn. Then, using a darning needle or bodkin and threading it with a length of thick wool, he may proceed to darn a fabric, reproducing one of the weave patterns shown in Chapter 1.

As the result of much tedious labour a small square of not very beautiful cloth will have been produced, but the following valuable lessons will have been learnt:

(a) Selecting the warp threads in the proper order is not only slow but, unless great care is taken in the counting, mistakes in the weave pattern will occur.

(b) If several coloured wefts are used we shall soon get them in a tangle and even if only one is used it is very difficult to lay it in a perfectly straight line from edge to edge. By the use of a coarse toothed comb for beating up the picks some degree of straightness will be achieved but, unless great care is taken to beat with constant force, the number of picks per inch will vary, and unless the weft is drawn across with constant tension the width of the cloth will vary and will show a distressing tendency to become progressively narrower.

(c) The warp threads will grow tighter as they become more and more interwoven until it becomes almost impossible to draw the weft across.

(d) However carefully we insert the teeth of the comb among the warp threads it will be impossible to ensure even distribution of the warp across the fabric. If we have used two colours of warp thread to produce stripes, this uneven distribution will show up by the stripes being of variable width.

(e) We shall have discovered that in weaving there are three basic actions which must be performed in sequence. Warp selection, known as shedding, weft insertion or picking, and weft placing or beating up.

A loom is therefore a machine which performs these three operations and so produces what Dr. Johnson described as 'Threads crossed and interlaced in perfectly expanded form'.

It is this performance of a complex series of operations whereby a fully fashioned article is produced at one stroke which differentiates the loom from other machines, most of which perform a single operation such as cutting, drilling or shaping of raw material, each machine contributing one bit to the end product, whereas each pick of a loom builds up one unit of pattern and it is by building pick upon pick that the complete design is formed.

The story of the evolution of the loom as we know it today falls into two parts. In the first stage there is the invention of mechanisms each performing one of the three basic operations but co-ordinated by the weaver's brain, hands and feet, while in the second stage the whole business is put under automatic control; not only is mechanical power used to replace man power in the literal sense of the term, but the machine is given a built-in memory by which it knows not only what operations to carry out but also the order in which to do so. When we realise that this memory technique and process control is the latest application of computer science to manufacture but that completely satisfactory solutions to all the problems had been produced before the end of the 18th century we shall appreciate how remarkable is the story of ingenuity we are studying. We must also remember that in the 18th century, engineering, as we use the word today, did not exist. The carpenter and the blacksmith were the fellow craftsmen who shared with the weaver the credit for a series of remarkable achievements.

The Making of a Warp

Reverting to the lessons we learnt from our darning experiment we recall that the first was that by the use of a frame loom we limited ourselves to a piece of fabric which could at best be a few feet long and this limitation also applied to the Peruvian back-strap loom in Plate 4.

The earliest method of making a long warp was to put a pair of pegs several yards apart and round these the warper by walking backwards and forwards unwound a bobbin of thread to form a parallel series containing the requisite total number of ends. When the warp had been built up to the required size it was detached from the pegs and rolled up on a wooden cylinder—this was the weaver's beam of antiquity. If this beam was put at the back of a strong frame and the warp drawn forward and attached to a roller for gathering up the woven cloth then the problem of almost unlimited length had been solved.

The next stage in warp making was the invention of the mill, which overcame two difficulties: it enabled much greater lengths to be used, and also—which was even more important—a number of supply bobbins could be used at the same time, thus cutting down the labour cost. Plate 9 shows a hand warping mill such as was in common use up to the end of the 19th century.

The essential parts of the mill were the creel (a) or bobbin frame from which the supply of yarn was drawn and the skeleton drum on which the warp was gradually built up, a section at a time. Each section was known as a portee and, as 20 bobbins was a convenient number, the unit of counting was the score.

The circumference of the drum varied from three to six yards and it was mounted on a vertical spindle and caused to rotate by a hand wheel and belt.

The most interesting part of the mechanism was the traversing block (b), mounted so as to rise or fall on two vertical bars, and it was the movement of this block which caused the warp to be laid as a spiral round the drum. This was done by a cord attached to the main spindle in such a way that it was wound or unwound as the drum rotated, the other end of the cord was attached to the block, not directly but through a rotatable peg which was kept in place by a ratchet. After one spiral of warp had been laid this ratchet peg was slightly twisted thus shortening the cord and this meant that the second spiral was laid alongside the first and not on top of it. Had the latter been the case, when the whole warp was unwound the outer layers would be slightly longer than the the inner ones and this would create uneven tension when the warp was put in the loom.

Hand warping was a most delicate and highly skilled art and the old saying, 'Well warped is half woven' shows its importance.

If the warper had merely piled portee on portee a tangled mass of threads would have been the result, so a method had to be devised whereby the threads were kept in perfect sequence and this was done by an operation known as 'Taking the Cross'. In Plate 9 it will be seen that the threads coming off the bobbins form a cone and can be numbered in sequence starting at the bottom right-hand corner and finishing at the top left-hand corner. Using his finger and thumb the warper picked out the threads so that all the odd numbers were in front of the thumb and behind the finger while the even numbers went the reverse way. This formed an 'X' pattern which was slipped on to two pegs at the bottom of the frame. When the complete warp had been built up the pegs were replaced by a thick cord, so that when the complete warp was unwound from the drum the threads would be in regular order for tying into the loom where the cross was permanently preserved by a pair of wooden rods.

Simple as it appears the whole operation was one calling for great delicacy of touch. Even the turning of the driving wheel was important because, unless the speed was kept absolutely constant, the bobbins would over-run and a slack section of warp would be laid.

There was one decorative effect which depended entirely on the warper's skill, the creation of shaded effects known as 'Ombre' stripes. These were delicately graduated tones of colour looking like the effect a water-colour painter produces by graduated washes, which may go simply from dark to light or may change completely from, say yellow, through tones of orange to red.

To produce this effect the dyer had to dye separate batches of yarn in a graduated series of dye baths each subtly different from the one before so that the series might be:

Red	Red/Orange	Orange	Yellow/Orange	Yellow
1, 2, 3, 4	5, 6, 7, 8	9, 10, 11, 12	13, 14, 15, 16	17, 18, 19, 20

However cunningly the dyer varied his shades, a warp made by the straightforward sequence 1–20 would show up when woven as stripes.   In order therefore to soften the boundaries the warper introduced zones of mixed threads so that the change from say Red 1 to Red 2 would be made by introducing a section where alternate bobbins of the two tones were used before going on to pure Red 2.

One of the most elaborate ombre's ever produced was the Victory Medal Ribbon given after the 1914–18 war.   A specimen of this can be bought at a military tailors and if examined will be found to cover the complete spectrum from deep violet at the edges passing through indigo and blue to green, yellow, orange to a vivid red in the centre.   Extremely fine threads were essential for this work and real silk of 40–44 denier was used and this had roughly 120,000 yards to the pound.

Dressing The Warp

When the complete warp was finished it was unwound in the form of a thick rope on to a roll for transport to the dressing frame, Plate 10, when it was rewound in expanded flat form on to a skellet which consisted of a series of fine steel pins driven into a bar of hard wood.   Another bar of wood formed a detachable cap for closing the top ends of the pins. The dresser had to space out the warp, putting a precalculated number of threads in each dent of the comb so that the total width was a little wider than that of the finished width of the fabric to be woven.   As the winding of the warp on to the beam proceeded, layers of hard but flexible paper were interleaved every so often in order to preserve an absolutely flat surface of constant diameter from edge to edge.   The reason for this was that as the warp unrolled during the weaving the slightest variation in diameter would pay off different lengths of yarn and this would show up in the woven cloth as shadow stripes.

Nowadays all this delicate and skilled hand work is done on automatic machines and warps are made and dressed in one operation. The old bobbin creel in which each bobbin only held about one ounce of yarn has been replaced by giant creels holding 1,000 or more cones of yarn and each supplying 30,000 yards of thread.

Tension is now automatically controlled and if a thread breaks, not only does the machine stop, but a signal light is switched on to indicate the position of the broken thread.

The taking of the cross is no longer a matter of good eyesight and delicate fingers; odd or even threads are separated mechanically.

Tension

Before weaving can begin the threads of the warp must be tightened and kept at an even tension throughout the length, which it will be noted has now grown from a few feet in our primitive loom to an almost indefinite length governed only by the maximum diameter of beam which can be accommodated.

If we fit across the front of the loom a roller which can take up the cloth as it is woven, then the problem of limited length has been overcome.

The simplest tension device is the band brake, formed by wrapping a piece of strong rope either round the beam itself or round a grooved flange; to one end of the rope is fixed a heavy weight which, but for the resistance of the warp threads would fall to the ground, winding the warp back on the beam; to the other end is fixed a small weight which serves only to give the rope a grip on the flange. As weaving proceeds the warp unwinds against the tension of the heavy weight until the small weight touches the floor and so relaxes the grip of the rope, whereupon the heavy weight slips back a fraction of an inch and in so doing lifts the small one clear of the floor. We have thus reached a position of equilibrium and the warp beam will now rotate against a force which remains constant within very fine limits. On modern power looms very elaborate and ingenious mechanisms are used, but most of them are developments of this ancient and simple idea.

Beating up the Weft

As long as a toothed comb was used for beating up the weft several serious problems remained unsolved. In the first place the use of the comb was a separate operation, involving laying down the shuttle and picking up another tool, secondly it was difficult to regulate the force of the blows needed to drive home the weft so that exact straightness was ensured and thirdly, the insertion and withdrawal of the comb would inevitably cause uneven distribution of the warp threads.

All these problems were solved by the twin inventions of the batten and the reed. The latter device, so called because it was originally made from fine slips of cane or bamboo, was a comb with closed teeth. By the even spacing of these teeth or dents as they are called and by threading a constant number of warp ends through each of them, even distribution could be achieved.

By mounting the reed on a strong bar of wood and by hanging this from rods pivoted at their upper end the whole device could be swung to and fro like a pendulum. The mass of the batten as the bar was called and its rigidity gave a hard blow to the weft and forced it into a straight line, while at the same time the reed being permanently in place on the warp ensured that at the exact moment of beat up each warp end was exactly in its correct place.

By mounting the batten off the vertical line it could be pushed back by the weaver's hand while he threw the shuttle when it would fall back by gravity to give its blow to the weft.

The reed (sometimes called a slay) was a beautiful piece of craftsmanship and Plate 14 shows how it was made. A pointed steel spike fitted with razor-edged fins was forced into a bamboo cane so as to split it into fine strips and these were flattened and gauged to exact thickness by an adjustable knife set close to a metal plate. The bamboo slips were then set between two rods and as each one was put into position a fine cord was wrapped round the rod. The thickness of this cord determined the number of slots or dents per inch. After assembly the ends were dipped in shellac varnish to cement the cords and the slips together.

So sensitive is the human eye that errors of a few thousandths of an inch in a reed will show as streaks in the fabric owing to the non-uniform distribution of the warp.

Fine and delicate as the reed is, it has to resist hard usage because the full force of the blow by which the weft is driven home is borne by the reed.

Today the bamboo and wooden rods and the shellac are replaced by steel and solder, but when it is realised that in a modern highspeed loom the reed may deliver as many as a 100,000 blows in a working day it will be appreciated that it is a small masterpiece of delicate engineering.

This arrangement of batten and reed was invented at a very early period and, when in course of time the power loom was evolved, it was a simple matter to replace the natural pendulum swing by a motion derived from a crank.

In the days of hand weaving the method was to make an inch or so of cloth and then to interrupt the weaving to wind it up by hand; but later on the winding up was done automatically by a ratchet wheel device which, through a chain of gears, caused the roll to turn by a fraction of an inch equal in amount to the space desired between two successive picks.

Warp Selection

As was pointed out in Chapter 1, the great basic weaves evolved thousands of years ago and still used today for most of the cloth which is woven, are very simple permutations of eight or less numbers so that even for the most elaborate of them, the satin, a warp containing a 1,000 ends will only be interlaced with the weft in eight different ways, i.e. the 1st, 9th, 17th, 25th and so on threads will behave exactly alike as will the 2nd, 10th, 18th and 26th. Therefore if each group can be attached to a bar which can be lifted at will, then eight bars will cover the full range of selection.

The whole apparatus is known as a harness and the control of each thread is effected by an eyelet in a cord known as a leish. Figure 10 shows how this arrangement works for the simplest of all weaves, ground, where odd/even and even/odd is the weave sequence.

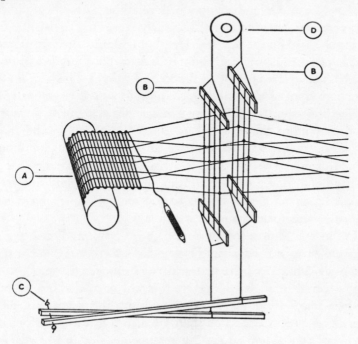

Figure 10. Warp selection

The fabric A is produced by working the treadles C so as to raise and lower the shafts BB (coupled together by a card working over pulley D) and through them separating the warp into two layers, between which the shuttle lays the weft.

Clearly all that we now have to do instead of laboriously counting out the warp ends is to raise or lower the shafts in such order as to form the desired sequence.

This can most simply be done by treadles, one for each shaft; but, for a rather interesting reason, these are not connected in the order 1–2–3–4 because the weaver would then have to treadle in a complex order, i.e. for a satin it would be 1–4–7–2–5–8–3–6, and this would be very distracting when his mind was also engaged on the other tasks of weft control and colour selection. So at a very early stage in the history of loom development the simple idea was evolved of cross-linking treadles to rhythm 1–3–2–4–5–7–6–8, a physically easy task by which the shafts would be worked in the desired order.

Very ingenious and elaborate developments were gradually evolved whereby rising and falling shafts were counterbalanced, so easing the load on the weaver's legs; but basically the essential step had been taken towards division of labour, the weaver had now got both hands free to ply his shuttle and, provided he kept up the simple rhythm of his treadling, continuous weaving was possible.

The limitations of this idea was the physical one of accommodating more than a small number of treadles in the space available. What was wanted was an automatic selector which would connect the shafts in rotation to a single treadle or pair of treadles so that a complex lifting order would only involve a simple, 1, 2, 1, 2, movement of the feet. This problem was solved by the invention of the Satin Jack.

In this mechanism the two treadles are connected to a pair of bars linked by a cord passing over pulleys so that as one bar rises the other falls. Each harness shaft was connected to a hook so that it could be inclined slightly forward or backwards from a vertical line. If in the forward position, the hook would be carried up and its associated shaft lifted, whereas those left in the back position would sink. An arrangement of link cords was made so that the shaft rising on the first pick would draw forward the hook required for the second pick and this in turn would select the third and so on; till, in an eight shaft weave the eighth shaft to lift would pull the first and so form a ring cycle of operations which would go on indefinitely.

Two features of this invention are important because they are the roots out of which two things grew. First, there was the idea of lifting shafts by means of a rising and falling bar, a principle which later formed one of the two main mechanisms of the Jacquard machine, and secondly, the idea of using link cords to form a built-in memory which would issue a chain of commands without any action on the part of the weaver.

The Draw Loom

All the shedding mechanisms so far described are excellent for the production of the basic weaves described in Chapter One, but these are textures rather than designs and so, if patterns are to be woven, and if we wish to avoid the tedious finger work of tapestry weaving, some method must be evolved whereby any warp end may be selected and lifted, not in some arithmetical sequence, but at the discretion of the designer. Even more important is the need for accurate repetition of a motif because a large area such as a curtain is decorated by multiple repeats of a small design unit.

Having translated his design on to squared paper to show how warp and weft intersect, the weaver then needs a memory device in which this information can be stored and from which it can be played back as many times as are necessary.

The answer to these problems was the Draw Loom shown in Plate 11 which is taken from an 18th-century print as may be judged from the dress of the workers, but the remarkable thing is that, from a study of ancient fabrics woven in China in pre-Christian times, and damasks woven in the Middle East and Italy as well as the rich brocades woven in Lyons and Spitalfields during the 17th and 18th centuries, we know that this complex mechanism was in common use all over the world and from very ancient times.

Despite its apparent complexity the machine works on a very simple principle which we can study by means of a piece of string stretched across a table, fixed at one end by a drawing pin and held tight by a small weight tied to the other end which hangs down over the end of the table. If we then take the horizontal part of the string and pluck it sideways it will be shortened in overall length and the weight will rise and if we imagine a small loop in the string placed just above the weight and through which a warp thread is passed then, when the string is drawn sideways, the warp thread will be lifted and so form a shed. If we have a great number of strings some means must be devised for plucking them in groups. Suppose therefore that out of

D

12 strings we wish to lift numbers 3, 7, 8, 11. This we can do by making four small loops of fine cord each encircling one of the desired strings and then tie the tails of the loops into a common knot so that when this is pulled up it will take with it all the attached loops.

Not only is this a mechanically convenient device but it is also a memory store, for if we go away for days and, when we come back, have forgotten the numbers of the strings which were to be lifted, no harm is done; a pull on the knot will lift the correct selection.

Figure 11 shows how this idea is applied in practice and for sake of clarity only nine warp ends and four picks are shown, the loops, properly called the simple, control the vertical cords— the tail—and by the shortening of these the appropriate warp threads are raised in the loom. However complicated the pattern, the worker has only to pull the simple in straight rotation so that an indefinite number of repeats, all identical, can be made. This rather elaborate apparatus had, for obvious reasons, to be placed outside the main frame of the loom and could not therefore be operated by the weaver himself but called for the services of a boy whose task it was to pluck the cords of the simple, keeping exactly in time with the weaver's movements.

The full significance of all the complex mechanisms in Plate 11 requires a little explanation, and from internal evidence we can make an intelligent guess about what was being woven.

In the first place there are two warps, the main one coming from the roll at the back and the other from the slanting frame which holds several hundred separate bobbins each tensioned by its own little weight hanging from a cord. There are also two harnesses, the first being an eight shaft plain one worked by treadles and levers operated by the weaver's feet, and the second is the draw-harness worked by the boy. Only one fabric would call for this arrangement, a rich satin plain cloth ornamented by a figured pile velvet, each thread of which must be able to draw off its own independent supply of thread determined by the way in which it weaves in the pattern.

The labour of setting up such a loom, which may well have

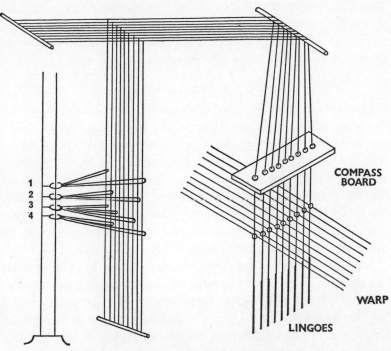

1
2
3
4

COMPASS
BOARD

WARP

LINGOES

Figure 11. The principle of the draw loom

had 10,000 warp threads, was enormous; but it had one good effect—these old hand weavers lavished their skill and time only on designs of great artistic merit, as anyone may see by visiting a museum.

When in the 19th century the Jacquard machine made it possible to change a pattern in an hour or so by merely replacing one pack of punched cards by another, the ease of production meant a proliferation of design with a corresponding fall in artistic quality. Complexity for its own sake became dominant until William Morris showed how textiles, if disciplined, could be a medium for the creative artist.

The immense amount of labour involved in draw loom weaving made figured material very costly and so in the 18th century when there came the outburst of inventive genius which found its first applications in the textile field there was a strong incentive to replace the draw loom by something automatic and to make it an integral part of the loom, so that the weaver himself could control all the motions. Thus do we come to the story of Bonchon, Vaucanson and finally Jacquard.

The Jacquard Machine

As so often happens in the history of invention one man's name becomes known to the public who forget those whose early efforts laid the groundwork on which others built. James Watt was not the originator of steam engines nor did Marconi invent wireless, they were brilliant practical engineers who produced the first commercially usable apparatus. So it was with Jacquard. As far back as 1725 Bonchon in France applied the idea of using paper perforated with holes as a means of selecting by needles those cords of a draw loom which were to be lifted.

In 1745 Vaucanson improved the mechanism by adding what is called the griffe, a bar of metal which by a crank was caused to rise and fall carrying with it those wires which had been selected by Bonchon's perforated paper. To Vaucanson must also go the credit for putting the whole apparatus on top of the loom, a position which it occupies today.

Born in 1752 at Lyons Jacquard took part in the French Revolution and, when the Peace of Amiens opened up communications with England, he read in a London newspaper of a prize being offered to anyone who could invent a machine for weaving net; this he succeeded in doing and gave a piece of material he had woven to a friend, but so little did Jacquard think of his invention that he forgot all about it until one day he was arrested on the orders of Napoleon and taken to Paris where he was interrogated by Napoleon himself and Carnot who asked 'Are you the man who pretends to do that which God Almighty cannot do, tie a knot in a stretched string?' He thereupon built a model of his device and so cleared himself of a charge of technological blasphemy. He was then asked to examine a loom, probably built on Vaucanson's principle, which had failed to weave satisfactorily certain rich fabrics for Bonaparte's personal use, and succeeded in producing a simple and satisfactory solution of the problem. He was rewarded by the grant of a pension of 1,000 crowns and sent home to Lyons where he was greeted with such hostility that on three occasions he barely escaped with his life. The Conseil des Prudhommes, who were the supervisors of the Lyons silk industry, ordered his machine to be broken up and, in Jacquard's own words, the wood was sold as wood and the iron as iron while the inventor was delivered over to universal ignominy.

So ended, for the moment, this early example of punched card automation as an aid to increased productivity.

Jacquard died in poverty in 1834 but the inhabitants of Lyons did not forget him because the employment of his machine brought great prosperity to the city; and so on the spot where his loom had been burnt they put a marble statue in his honour.

The basic principle of the Jacquard machine is very simple although the thing itself looks bewilderingly complicated, containing as it does hundreds of needles, hooks and springs. Figure 12 shows the essential working parts for four warp ends A, B, C,

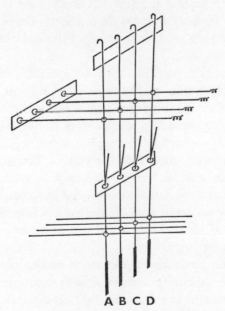

A B C D

Figure 12. The principle of the Jacquard

D, each of which is controlled by a leish suspended from a wire hook which is controlled by a needle that has twisted in it a small eye. These needles, which are horizontal, are kept pushed forward by small springs and their front ends are supported by being passed through a perforated board, known as the needle board. From this they project about a quarter of an inch and against these projecting needles is pressed a stiff card in which holes are perforated opposite the needles and hooks which are lifted.

The effect of pressing the card against the needles is to push back those which are to stay down and leave in a forward position those which are to rise. Running along below each row of hooks is a bar, known as the griffe, which rises and falls by means of crank mechanisms, so carrying with it the hooks which need to be lifted, thus forming a shed in which any desired selection of warp ends can be created.

The perforated cards, each of which represents one pick, are laced together in an endless chain and pass over a square cylinder which makes a quarter turn at every pick thus bringing a new card into the operating position. The cylinder is like a honeycomb having as many holes as there are needles in the machine, so that where there is a hole in the card the end of the needle can pass freely through.

At one side of the machine are a few special hooks and needles which control various mechanisms of the loom such as weft selection and the take down rollers. Thus it is possible not only to translate any pattern into fabric but to decide which of several wefts is to weave on any particular pick and to regulate how many picks per inch will be put into the cloth. Thus quality, colour and design are brought under complete automatic control. So perfect was Jacquard's solution of all the problems involved that even today, apart from purely mechanical improvements, this machine is used all over the world just as he invented it over a century and a half ago.

The amazing thing about this story of the evolution of the loom from the primitive Peruvian back strap idea to the fully automated Jacquard loom is that engineering and science, as we today use the terms, played no part; everything was done by the ingenuity of craftsmen working in wood, metal and thread who by their partnership gave us so much that is both useful and beautiful.

The coming of the Jacquard loom brought into existence a new craft skill—the art of the textile designer, a man who must combine the ability of the artist, who understands shape and colour, with that of the weaver who knows how warp and weft must be united in conformity with the laws of good fabric structure. Although it is possible in theory to select even one warp end out of several thousand, it is still necessary to do this in such a way that the final result is a cloth which will be at once firm and flexible and suitable for a definite purpose. Like other industrial designers, the textile designer is one who must work within a strict discipline; taste and technology must go hand in hand.

Taking the artist's original painting the designer must therefore be able to show what is to happen at each intersection of warp and weft. He therefore takes a sheet of squared paper about three feet wide and four feet long and enlarges the design to such a size that each warp thread is represented by a vertical row of squares and each pick by an horizontal row, so that each small square represents an intersection at which, as we saw in Chapter 1, only one of two things is possible—warp lies over weft or weft is over warp. The designer is able to show exactly how each thread behaves at each point of the design.

When the design has been painted on the squared paper, this is handed to the stamper who with the aid of a piano machine—so called because keys control punches—punches the card which represents one pick of weft of one colour all across the fabric. When several colours of weft are used, each one is read off on to a separate card which is also stamped with the appropriate code holes to bring the correct shuttle into operation. In brocade weaving the wefts are not bound closely enough to make a firm fabric nor of course does any colour weave all across the cloth, therefore, a base fabric is wanted; this is provided by what is called a ground card which (inserted at the start of each colour sequence) sends the ground shuttle from edge to edge interweaving all the warp threads in taffeta, twill or satin. Plate 16 shows the connection between cards and shuttles for multi-colour work.

It should be pointed out that in order to economise space the needles of the machine are set in rows of 6 or 12 so that a 600-needle machine is set in 50 rows of 12 needles. The stamper reads off a row at a time and, in order to help him to do this, the squared paper is over-ruled by heavy lines every 6 or 12 threads.

Picking

As soon as the first simple shedding mechanism had been invented, the laborious darning of the weft ceased to be necessary, and the way was open for the evolution of the shuttle which consisted of a smooth torpedo-shaped piece of hard wood having a large cavity in which a spool of weft could be inserted. This could be thrown from side to side of the cloth paying off yarn as it went. Like the arrow which we now realise is a masterpiece of aerodynamic design, the shuttle is the perfect answer to the problem of weft control. Over thousands of years it has remained almost unchanged.

Thrown from hand to hand—and this limited the width of cloth a weaver could make by himself—the shuttle was the essential tool of his craft.

Until 1733 the weaver's productivity was limited by the speed with which he could throw the shuttle across the warp; but in that year came the first of the great textile inventions; Henry Kay invented the fly shuttle which speeded up and eased production not only because it flew across the loom faster than was possible by hand, but also because the flight path was straight and moreover only one hand was required for picking, leaving the other one free for beating up the reed.

The fly shuttle is shown in Plate 13. It consists of boxes at either end of the batten, each of which is fitted with a hammer block or picker sliding freely on a metal rod. The two hammers are linked by a cord which can be jerked in either direction, so giving a sharp blow to the shuttle which flies across into the opposite box. Even in the modern power loom this basic idea is still used although the hammers are operated by cam mechanisms.

A logical improvement to Kay's idea was the drop box whereby several shuttles each carrying a different coloured weft could be worked at will. This is a box, fitted with two or more shelves, on which a shuttle rested, which could be raised and lowered independently so as to bring the desired shuttle in line with the pickers.

The Shuttleless Loom

Like any other device the shuttle had its weaknesses and inventors have made many ingenious attempts to overcome them. The greatest drawback to the shuttle is its limited capacity since it must, because of the size of the shed, be slender and, because it is thrown like a projectile, it must be as light as possible. This means that at frequent intervals a new pirn or quill of yarn must be inserted and, in order to do this, either the loom must be stopped or an elaborate mechanical change mechanism must be used. The ideal, therefore, would be a weightless yarn carrier drawing its supply from a large package; and to achieve this three methods have been put forward.

The first is the needle or rapier loom, in which the shuttle is replaced by a long thin needle having an eye in its point through which the weft is threaded. The needle is thrust across the shed and the yarn is caught and held while the needle is withdrawn, leaving behind a double loop of weft.

The second idea might be described as the machine-gun; it is loaded with small bullets of weft, which are fired across the shed paying out a tail of yarn as they go. When each bullet reaches the opposite side of the warp the tail is cut off and the bullets are carried back by a conveyor and reloaded into the gun. Provided the magazine is kept replenished with bullets, this enables the loom to run for an indefinite period and very high speeds can be attained because the moving mass is so small; also a very narrow shed can be used thus easing the strain on the warp.

The third and latest development employs a device which resembles the schoolboy's water pistol and consists of a powerful little pump which squirts a fine jet of water across the open shed. If weft is available from an almost tensionless supply and is brought in contact with a jet, it will be carried along, and so a pick is laid and this is caught and held by fine tweezers, the tail end being cut off by scissors operated by a cam mechanism.

Although this leaves a fringe of cut ends down the selvedges of the cloth, this is not an objection because they are cut off when it is used by garment makers. Here we combine the advantages of endless yarn supply, small moving mass and a very small shed. The two weaknesses are that only very fine and light yarn can be carried by jets and this must be one of the man-made fibres such as Nylon and Terylene which are highly water repellent by nature; cotton and wool have a high water affinity and so become waterlogged.

This revolutionary idea is now used commercially and speeds as high as 400 picks per minute are commonly reached. Anybody seeing a battery of these water jet looms running will immediately be struck by the fact that they are almost noiseless— the simile of the 'busy clack of the weaver's shuttle' has gone and has been replaced by a low humming sound, but as the hum of bees is also synonymous with virtuous activity, the literary and moral aspects of the matter are not affected.

Apart from the digression into rapiers, machine-guns and water pistols we have traced the story of the evolution of the loom to the end of its first chapter, in which one by one the difficulties and limitations of the primitive hand frame and darning technique have been overcome by ingenious mechanisms; but the weaver is still the source of power to drive the loom and it is his brain which must co-ordinate the various movements required for the three operations of shedding, picking and beating up.

Plate 12 shows the hand loom in its fully developed form, all the operations were mechanically performed by muscle power and the synchronisation of the movements still depended on the worker himself.

The Evolution of the Power Loom

Most inventors are practical men whose experience shows them what problems require solution, but one exception was a clergyman, Dr. Edmund Cartwright. Educated at University College

Oxford, he was presented to the living of Goadby Marwood in Leicestershire. Here he might well have lived out his days in virtuous obscurity had he not gone on a visit to Matlock.

Many years later he wrote a letter to his friend Mr. Bannatyne and so we have the story in his own words:

'Happening to be at Matlock in the summer of 1784, I fell in company with some gentlemen of Manchester, when the conversation turned on Arkwright's spinning machinery. One of the company observed, that as soon as Arkwright's patent expired so many mills would be erected, and so much cotton spun, that hands could never be found to weave it. To this observation I replied that Arkwright must then set his wits to work to invent a weaving mill. This brought on a conversation on the subject, in which the Manchester gentlemen unanimously agreed that the thing was impracticable; and in defence of their opinion they adduced arguments which I certainly was incompetent to answer, or even to comprehend, being totally ignorant of the subject, never having at any time seen a person weave. I controverted, however, the impracticability of the thing, by remarking that there had lately been exhibited in London an automaton figure which played chess. "Now you will not assert, gentlemen," said I, "that it is more difficult to construct a machine that shall weave, than one which shall make all the variety of moves which are required in that complicated game."

'Some little time afterwards a particular circumstance recalling this conversation to my mind, it struck me that, as in plain weaving, according to the conception I then had of the business, there could only be three movements, which were to follow each other in succession, there would be little difficulty in producing and repeating them. Full of these ideas I immediately employed a carpenter and smith to carry them into effect. As soon as the machine was finished, I got a weaver to put in the warp, which was of such materials as sail cloth is usually made of. To my great delight a piece of cloth, such as it was, was the produce. As I had never before turned my thoughts to anything mechanical, either in theory or practice, nor had ever seen a loom at work, or knew anything of its construction you will readily suppose that my first loom was a most rude piece of machinery. The warp was placed perpendicularly, the reed fell with the weight of at least half a hundredweight, and the springs which threw the shuttle were strong enough to throw a Congreve rocket. In short, it required the strength of two powerful men to work the machine at a slow rate, and only for a short time. Conceiving, in my simplicity, that I had accomplished all that was required, I then secured what I thought a most valuable property by a patent—4th April, 1785. This being done, I then condescended to see how other people wove; and you will guess my astonishment, when I compared their easy modes of operation with mine. Availing myself, however, of what I then saw I made a loom, in its general principles nearly as they are now made. But it was not till the year 1787 that I completed my invention, when I took out my last weaving patent, August 1st in that year.'

What a fantastic story it is; a clergyman with no mechanical knowledge overhears an economic argument and goes away and produces a solution to the problem. Before we indulge in a superior smile at the Doctor's self-revelation let us consider what were the difficult engineering problems for which he had to find a solution, then and only then can we fully appreciate the stature of this almost forgotten genius.

What Cartwright and his successors had to do was to replace the hands and feet of the weaver by mechanisms which, drawing their motive power from a revolving crank, could break it up into separate parts and motions all co-ordinated in the proper sequence, and this they did by the use of cams which in essence are a means of converting rotary motion into push-pull action.

To trace all this in detail would take us into the history of textile invention in the 19th and 20th centuries and would need a book for its full story; but as so often happens the traditional originator of anything is discovered to have had his forerunners, Hero of Alexandria designed a jet propulsion engine long before Sir Frank Whittle was born. So in the case of automatic weaving we find that the Dutch Engine or as it is sometimes called the 'A-La-Bar' Loom was a prior solution of the problems which

Cartwright had to solve. It is the ribbon weavers rather than the broadloom weavers who were the pioneers.

The adjectives 'multi-spindle' and 'automatic' are so typical of 20th-century machinery that it comes as a surprise to find a book published in Venice in 1636 saying that one Anthony Möller of Danzig had, fifty years previously, seen a machine on which four to six pieces could be woven at the same time, but that the council, fearing that it would cause unemployment among the weavers had caused the inventor to be privately strangled or drowned. The next reference to this idea was in 1641 when we hear of the use of such a machine in Leyden but once again the authorities prohibited its use and had to suppress rioting among the workers; and again in 1685 the Council of Frankfort forbad its use and the Council of Hamburg ordered the loom to be publicly burnt. In spite of all this persecution the machine was so obviously useful that it became popular and, in an encyclopedia published in France in 1786, it is described and illustrated and spoken of as being in common use. In 1785 the loom was in use in England and Henry Kay and his partner John Stell of Keighley took out a patent for improvements to the Dutch Engine.

The driving force behind this series of inventions was the fact that by foot treadling and the hand-throwing of the shuttle the hand loom could only be worked at a fixed speed which was independent of the width of the work and so, for a narrow fabric such as ribbon, the cost of production was disproportionately high. Plate 15 is based on the illustration in the French encyclopedia of 1786 and this clearly shows the construction.

Here we have ten separate warps the shedding of which was controlled by a common harness operated by tappets while the shuttles were driven by a pair of cams. Ten separate shuttles were mounted on a common batten, each having a limited motion across a single warp. The woven fabric was drawn down by rollers and carried to the back of the loom where it was coiled down in boxes. The motive power was the bar running across the front of the loom and this was pushed up and down by the weaver. Kay and Stell in their patent say that the loom may be worked by 'hands water or any other force', so clearly they had substituted some sort of crank for the weaver's hands.

All this represents a very sophisticated piece of design which must have been widely known; but there is no reason to suppose that Cartwright had any idea of what had already been done.

One very interesting feature of the drawing should be noted, it represents a magnificent example of the woodworker's art. Frames were usually made of pitch pine but the batten was mahogany and the shuttles of box wood whose close grain could be brought to an exceptionally fine finish. The slides or landings on which the shuttles ran were made of apple wood which had exceptional resistance to frictional wear.

Quite naturally the carpenters used the strongest construction they knew for the main frame, and so the form of members meeting at right angles and joined by a mortise and tenon joint was adapted.

When in the 19th century looms began to be made of iron the engineers failed to see that this rectangular construction was no longer necessary but as it could easily be reproduced in cast iron, they adopted the old shape. Hence textile machinery retained an antique look for no particular reason, although from an engineering point of view it had serious weaknesses, especially if high speeds were to be reached. Only within the last twenty-five years have designers broken away from tradition and have re-designed the loom in streamlined form by the intelligent use of modern materials and engineering techniques.

The same thing was seen in the motor car industry where bodywork long continued to be based on the old coach builders' shapes, the idea of forming a body out of pressed sheet metal came at a relatively late stage of the evolutionary story.

CHAPTER FOUR

The Weaver's Raw Materials

BEFORE men could weave there were many purposes for which thread was invaluable and so there was an incentive to discover something better than the sinews of animals or strips of leather; hence it is that one of the commonest domestic tools found by archaeologists is the pierced stone ring used as a spindle whorl for the spinning of thread.

The weaver's raw materials fall into three broad classes: first, continuous filaments of great length, such for example as real silk and the man-made yarns; secondly, fibres derived like cotton from the hairy coating of a seed pod or from the fleece of an animal such as the sheep or camel; and thirdly by materials such as linen and jute, obtained from the tough fibres found in the stems of certain plants such as flax, which, when separated from the pulpy tissue, can be spun into thread.

Today when transport makes all materials ubiquitous, we tend to overlook the fact that primitive societies had to adapt themselves, and develop soil and climate as provided in various parts of the world. The Chinese were, for thousands of years, users of silk because the mulberry trees, on which silk worms are fed, flourish naturally in their country; while in Egypt, Peru and India the cotton bush grows naturally and, in the temperate and cold zones, animals such as the sheep play a major part in the economy.

Everywhere however the basic problem was the same, how to convert the raw material furnished by nature into smooth strong uniform thread using filaments of extreme fineness and delicacy. The degree of skill required may be better appreciated if we consider the size of the filaments spun by the silk worm, or by man in the case of Rayon or Nylon, or a single fibre of cotton as it grows on the bush, all of which are of the same order of magnitude, 9,000 metres weighing between 2 and 5 grams. When such objects are measured under a microscope the micron, one thousandth of a millimeter, is the unit of measurement.

In the sections which follow, each material and its methods of preparation is described, but common to all is the delicacy of manipulation which is involved.

Anyone who goes for a country walk may find a tuft of wool on a hedgerow, and from the description given may, with the aid of a penknife, make a simple distaff and so proceed to spin a few feet of thread; after this instructive adventure he will better appreciate the significance of the fact that Indian muslins and oriental silks have been made so fine that a piece of fabric a yard wide can be drawn through a finger ring; while the cotton, spun in Lancashire, from which lawn is woven, is so fine that a pound would contain over a third of a million yards.

Silk

Chinese history records that Si Ling, wife of the Emperor Huang Ti, who lived in 2640 B.C. was the first patroness of the silk industry; not only did she encourage others, but she herself cared for silkworms and also invented the loom.

For many centuries the art of sericulture was a jealously guarded secret which the Chinese succeeded in protecting. Not till the 3rd century A.D. did a party of Koreans discover the art which they introduced to Japan. Legends tell how the first silkworm eggs were carried to India in the turban of a Chinese princess who married an Indian prince.

As the Roman Empire grew in wealth silk became a precious article of luxury and literally was worth its weight in gold; this caused the Emperor Justinian to make efforts to get eggs of what Aristotle had described as 'A great worm with horns'. After a number of unsuccessful efforts, two Persian monks were found who had visited China and become familiar with the methods of rearing silkworms; they were persuaded to go back and to try to secure some of the eggs and this they finally did by hiding them in the hollow bamboo staffs which supported their steps

1. 18TH-CENTURY BROCADE WEAVING, Chinese Draw Loom Work. Woven in pure silk these panels illustrate the quality of workmanship and intricacy of detail achieved on hand looms. *Victoria & Albert Museum, Crown Copyright.* T 39–1916

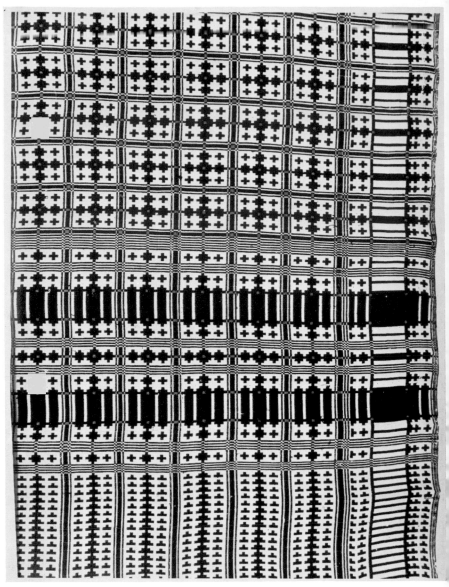

2. HAND-LOOM WEAVING, Muzaffarnagar, India. These complex geometrical designs are produced by a very simple mechanism on hand looms. Patterns of this type were produced in the colonial period of the U.S.A.

Victoria & Albert Museum, Crown Copyright. 4838 IS

3. HAND-WOVEN TAPESTRY. This design by William Morris is known as the 'Orchard Pattern'. Note particularly the exquisite detail in the foreground flowers.

Victoria & Albert Museum, Crown Copyright. 154–1898

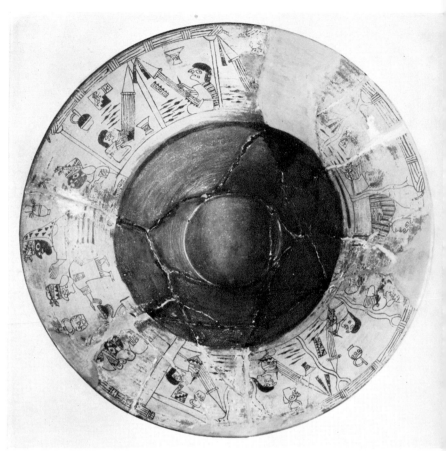

4. PERUVIAN WEAVERS AT WORK, *c.* 2000 B.C. Each weaver has a pattern on the wall corresponding in each case with the woven cloth. The number of colours can be determined by the number of shuttles used by the weaver. Note the two people serving drinks to the workers.   *British Museum*

5. CHARLOTTE, COUNTESS OF DERBY, probably by Gilbert
Jackson, 1635. Apart from the magnificent hand-made lace, note the
delicacy of the ribbon bows and the richness of the chair upholstery.
From the form of the highlights in the background drapery it is probable
that this was taffeta.

Victoria & Albert Museum, Crown Copyright. 565–1882

6. PILE FABRIC. Persian Carpet, 16th–17th century. Woven by hand, this has 300 knots per square inch. The vigour of the border design is exceptional.

Victoria & Albert Museum, Crown Copyright. 453–1884

7. CHINESE FRONTAL, Silk, 18th century. This is not only a masterpiece of hand weaving but a fine example of Chinese design. In the original the delicacy of the colours shows the skill of the dyers of the period.

Victoria & Albert Museum, Crown Copyright. T 273–1910

8. TAPESTRY WOVEN PANEL, Asia Minor, 5th century. The brilliance of the colours after a lapse of 1,500 years may be deduced from the strong tonal contrasts. The background fabric has been ornamented with loop work.

Victoria & Albert Museum, Crown Copyright. 275–1891

9. HAND WARPING MILL. Yarn was drawn from the bobbins in the creel (a) and wound on to the frame turned by the handle and pulley. The group of threads known as a portee was placed spirally by the rise and fall of the block (b). The worker is taking the cross which he will transfer from his fingers to the pegs (pp).

10. DRESSING THE WARP. The warp from the mill in Plate 9 is wound on to the drum. By the use of the comb or skellet the worker spreads the warp out to the cloth width. It is then wound on to the weaver's beam ready for insertion in the loom.

11. THE DRAW LOOM, 18th century. Probably invented in China in classical times, it spread to Asia Minor and thence to Europe at the time of the Crusades. The weaver operated the shuttle and the batten and, by the treadles, made the ground fabric. The boy, by plucking the draw cords, controlled the pattern. Brocade wefts would be used when the draw cords were operated. The fact that a main warp from a beam and a second warp from the creel were used indicates that a figured pile fabric was being woven.

12.　OUTDOOR WEAVER'S WORKSHOP.　This drawing from an old print shows a domestic weaving shop typical of those found in Spitalfields, Coventry and Macclesfield.　The necessity for good light and a lofty ceiling caused them to be built as attic rooms.

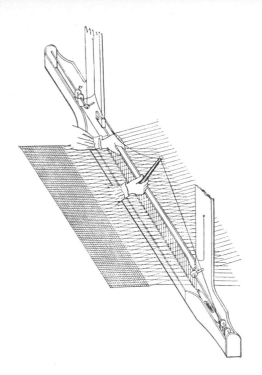

13. THE FLY SHUTTLE. Suspend[ed]
by two rods the batten carried the reed a[nd]
had at each end a box fitted with a slidi[ng]
hammer block which could be jerked by t[he]
cords attached to the stick. Single-hand[ed]
operation was secured and the shuttle cou[ld]
be propelled across greater distances th[an]
when thrown from hand to hand.

14. THE REED OR SLAY. The pointed
spike carrying small cutters was pushed into
a bamboo rod thus producing slips, afterwards reduced to proper thickness by a
cutting gauge. The slips were fixed into
upper and lower bars and suitably spaced by
the binding cord. By passing an appropriate number of warp ends through each
gap or dent a uniform distribution was
ensured.

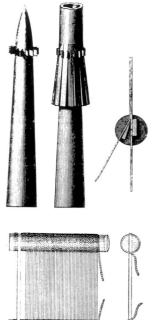

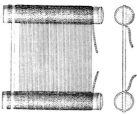

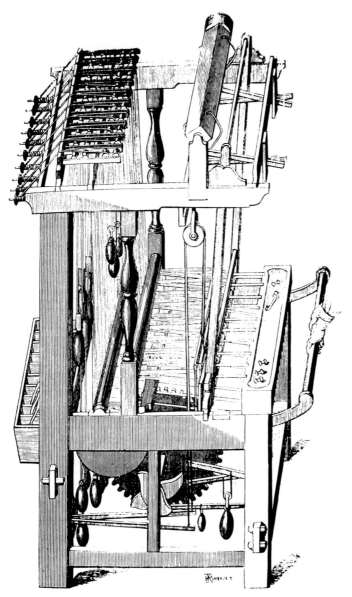

15. *A LA BAR*, or DUTCH ENGINE LOOM. Invented in Europe in the early 17th century this device not only enabled ten ribbons to be woven at one operation but produced and co-ordinated all the necessary movements from the motion of a single lever. Its similarity to a modern multi-shuttle loom is remarkable.

16. Fig. 1 (above left): The artist's sketch of a design to be reproduced in a woven fabric. Fig. 2 (right): The textile draftsman's drawing on squared paper made from the artist's sketch.   Only that part of the sketch within the small square on Fig. 1 is reproduced here because the drawing must be on a scale large enough to enable each small square to represent one thread of one colour.   It is the combination of different weaves in coloured yarns which produced the required design.   From this drawing the Jacquard cards are cut. Fig. 3 (lower left): A photograph of the fabric produced from the drawing in Fig. 2.   Each colour on the squared draft would be read off separately on to its own card so that a succession of colour picks could be obtained.

SPINNING WHEEL. Developed
m the hand-operated spindle it was
e forerunner of the mule.
Science Museum, London

18. SPINNING WHEEL. The use of the
flyer for putting in the twist continuously made
this the forerunner of the ring spinning frames.
Leonardo da Vinci's notebooks show a design
for this device which is extremely modern in
conception.   *Science Museum, London*

19. THE HELMSHORE JENNY. A modern replica built exactly to Hargreaves' specification at TMM (Research) Ltd., works. Valuable experiments have been made with this model. The low position of the handle shows why the machine was described as 'suitable for operation by children'. *TMM (Research) Ltd.*

across the deserts and mountains of Asia. Established first as a royal monopoly, silk production and weaving spread from Byzantium and Asia Minor and thence into the Mediterranean countries, becoming in course of time a great source of wealth to Italy and France.

Anxious to develop a native silk industry in Britain, James I offered a bounty to those who were willing to plant mulberry trees on which silkworms feed but, by a sad error in botany, he distributed the wrong species of tree and so the venture came to nought. Undiscouraged by this first failure he urged the settlers in Virginia to take up sericulture by propaganda which broke into verse:

> Where worms and food do naturally abound
> A gallant silken trade must there be found.
> Virginia excels the world in both—
> Envie nor malice can gaine say this troth.

Nothing came of this, but the Americans refused to give up the struggle and during the 19th century several attempts were made to establish the mulberry tree in the U.S.A. In 1838 Samuel Whitmarsh persuaded his fellow Pennsylvanians to plant yet another species of mulberry (*Morus multicaulis*) and so persuasive was he that 300,000 dollars were paid in a single week for trees and for a few years a speculative boom raged; but all was in vain, silkworms were resolute conservatives and remained faithful to their traditional diet of *Morus alba*. Even if James I and Mr. Whitmarsh got their botany right their ventures were doomed, because of all the creatures man has domesticated the silkworm calls for the most intense care and attention, and only in countries where low-paid peasant labour is abundant can silk be produced economically.

The silkworm is the caterpillar (Figure 13) of a moth, *Bombyx mori* (Figure 14), which is one of a group of insects that protect their chrysalids by wrapping them in a fibrous cocoon. After hatching from the egg the silkworm passes through four stages, pausing to shed its skin at the end of each. The final stage, called by the French 'Le grand gorge' is indeed an orgy during which the worm, having reached full size is now building up its silk glands.

E

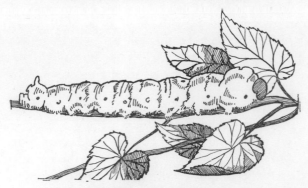

Figure 13. The Silkworm; about 3 inches long

Figure 14. The Silk Moth

Some idea of the voracity of the silkworm's appetite can be got when it is realised that the worms from one ounce of egg will eat about a ton of leaves during their growth period and of this total 1,800 pounds are eaten in the last stage, which involves stripping the leaves from a quarter of an acre of land.

When it is ready to begin spinning its coccon, the worm grasps a twig with its hind legs and by a rhythmic swaying of its body exudes liquid silk from two small holes in its head, thus laying the thread in a figure-of-eight pattern. As soon as it comes in contact with the air the silk hardens and, as its surface is coated with a natural gum, the layers of the cocoon are bonded together into a firm structure so light and bulky that two tons of cocoons fill a 10-ton railway wagon.

Like all creatures which have been the subject of selective breeding for economic reasons, the silkworm is a delicate thing and the greatest care has to be exercised at all stages of its life if it is to be reared successfully.

In certain parts of India, notably the province of Assam, a wild silkworm exists which lives on the foliage of trees from which the natives collect the cocoons. Owing to the diet on which the worms feed the silk they produce is rough in texture and stained a natural beige colour which it is difficult to bleach out; it is, however, exceptionally strong and durable and under the name Tussah or Tussore is highly esteemed for lightweight clothing.

The delicate constitution of the *Bombyx mori* was startlingly illustrated during the 1850–60 period when the disease known as pebrine broke out in France where silk production had grown to form an important part of the national economy. Within a few years the production had fallen to only a seventh of its former size and it looked as though the silk industry might be utterly destroyed. In 1865 the government became so alarmed that they sent a scientist to investigate the problem; his name was Louis Pasteur and after two years of patient investigation he found not only the cause of the disease, but how to control it. Apart from the value of his work in stamping out pebrine, Pasteur was helped in his wider work of bacterial infection by the experience he gained, and years afterwards when he had become internationally famous he said to those who came to be trained in his laboratories, 'Read the studies on the silkworm; it will be, I think, a good preparation for the investigation we are about to undertake'.

At first sight, nature having furnished him with thread in continuous lengths of many hundreds of yards, it might seem that the weaver's problems were solved; but two difficulties had to be overcome before cocoon silk was in a condition suitable for weaving. In the first place the thread spun by the silkworm is so fine that 16 or 24 filaments had to be cabled together in order to make even the finest weaving thread and secondly the filament was coiled up in a tight ball, firmly bound by the natural gum. Two new craftsmen therefore appear in the story—the reeler who unwraps the cocoons and the throwster who combines the filaments into yarn.

If the silkworm were left to its own devices, the chrysalis

when it hatched out into a moth would find itself imprisoned inside the cocoon through which it would eat its way out, and in so doing chop the silk into short lengths; hence as soon as the cocoons have formed, the creatures are killed by heat, only those needed for breeding purposes being allowed by the sericulturist to emerge naturally. About eight cocoons are then dropped into a bowl of hot water on the surface of which they float and the gum becomes softened. The worker then strokes them with a heather twig which picks up the ends of the filaments and enables them to be attached to a spider wheel on which they are wound. As the cocoons are free to bob about in a virtually frictionless condition the thread unwinds easily and its delicacy is no longer a difficulty. Great skill and judgement are called for in reeling and, although engineers have devoted much attention to the problem of mechanisation, it remains even today predominantly a hand process.

The thread produced by the reeler from his eight cocoons is too fine for the weaver and also suffers from the defect that the filaments are parallel to one another and are too soft to resist abrasion; hence it is necessary to subject the yarn to a twisting process in order to increase its durability and also to combine two or three threads together—all this is the work of the throwster. The mechanism he uses is shown in Figure 15 and consists of two bobbins, one placed on a vertical spindle capable of being rotated at high speed and the other on a horizontal spindle revolving more slowly; the thread is drawn by the second bobbin from the first through an 'S'-shaped wire mounted on the vertical spindle about which it is free to revolve independently or, if desired, may be carried round when the spindle rotates. The delicate adjustment of the friction between the spindle and the flyer as the 'S'-shaped wire is called, is the essence of this device. If the horizontal bobbin only is rotated, yarn will be wound up unchanged and the flyer will slowly turn, pulled round by the unwrapping of the thread; if, however, only the vertical bobbin is rotated then the effect will be to put twist in the thread, and the flyer will be carried round with the spindle. When both bobbins are rotated simultaneously the effect is twofold, the thread is

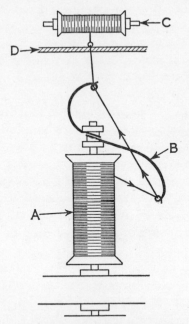

Figure 15. The throwing spindle

The vertical spindle A revolving rapidly carries with it, by friction only, the flier B, which transfers the thread onto the slowly revolving bobbin C. The bar D traverses the thread uniformly on C.

wound from bobbin to bobbin and twist is also inserted and, if several threads have been wound together on the first bobbin, they will be twisted into a cable.

This twisting and cabling of yarn is a vital stage in the preparatory processes of weaving, as the degree of twist governs in large measure the properties of the final cloth; tensile strength, uniformity and resistance to abrasion are all increased by twist, and as was pointed out in Chapter 1, overtwisting is the secret of crêpe effects.

In modern factories and wherever silk has been replaced by man-made fibres, the ring spinning frame has replaced the throwster's spindle, but the basic principle of two bobbins rotating at different speeds and interconnected by what is really a slipping clutch, remains the same.

By whatever standard we judge it, silk deserves its proud title of 'Queen of Fibres'; fine and delicate yet strong and hard wearing, light but warm and soft to the touch and, to the dyer, the finest medium on which he can exercise his skill.   It never-theless is declining steadily in importance as a material for the weaver, and for this sad situation three reasons can be given. First, the great amount of hand labour and skill involved at every stage makes silk fabric too costly for anything but luxury goods; secondly, being a natural product it is variable from season to season and from batch to batch and for these and other technical reasons does not lend itself to automatic large-scale production; thirdly, the rapid growth in world population with its increasing pressure on food resources means that land and labour must be diverted from the growing of mulberry trees to food production.

Man-Made Fibres

Silk, like gold, having always enjoyed a high scarcity value, naturally was the object of attention by alchemists who sought to transmute base materials into noble ones and so the idea of pene-trating the silkworm's secret was an attractive one.   The man who stood at the point in time when old alchemy was evolving into new science and technology was Robert Hooke who in his book *Micrographia*, written in 1664, discussed the problem of converting vegetable matter into silk.

The *Encyclopaedia Britannica* dismisses Hooke with unusual asperity saying, 'Hooke's scientific achievements would have been more striking if they had been less varied.   He originated much, but perfected little.   ... Hooke had an irritable temper, his habits were penurious and solitary.'

Wightman in his *Growth of Scientific Ideas* treats Hooke with the respect he deserves as one of that band of men who in the second half of the 17th century, broke out of the constricting bonds of mediaeval natural philosophy derived from Aristotle, and showed that by the application of scientific methods the way lay open to new and exiting discoveries.   Hooke and his friend Boyle, described on his tombstone as 'Father of Chemistry and Uncle of the Earl of Cork', were leaders of this movement and to them must be given proper credit for the creation of modern chemistry which furnished the tools wherewith others solved the problems of man-made and synthetic materials.

Two hundred years after Hooke, a young French chemist, Chardonnet, was assisting Pasteur in his researches in silkworm disease which threatened the silk industry with extinction, and he turned his attention to the problem of artificial silk. Armed with the necessary chemical knowledge he saw that the fundamental problem was to take cellulose which was cheap and plentiful, dissolve it so as to form a viscous fluid, and extrude it through a jet similar to the silkworm's spinnerette and then to solidify the resultant thread, either by chemical treatment or by evaporating the solvent.

Chardonnet chose as the basis of his process the principle that cellulose after treatment with nitric acid is changed into nitro-cellulose which is soluble in an alcohol-ether mixture; this solution, after extrusion, forms a silk-like thread when the solvents are removed. As seems to happen so often when a problem is in the air, others were working on parallel lines and so there were evolved in the last years of the 19th century four main processes of manufacture. In the Bemberg method Schweitzer's reagent, a copper ammonia compound, was the solvent, while the work of Swan and Bevan relied on the fact that cellulose after treatment with alkali and carbon bi-sulphide can be converted into a viscous fluid (known as viscose) which after extrusion and treatment with acid forms a clear strong filament; finally there was the acetate process which involved the treatment of vegetable fibre (cotton linters) with acetic acid, so making it soluble in acetone, from which solution threads can be spun.

For some years all four methods were exploited commercially, but gradually the viscose process, taken up by Courtaulds, proved the most successful, largely because the raw material, wood pulp, and the chemicals used were cheap and expendable, and so today in all countries the viscose process is the dominant one. Technical and economic problems for which no really satisfactory solution could be found caused the gradual decline of the Chardonnet and Bemberg processes.

All four types of rayon resembled silk in appearance, although they did not equal it in fineness or strength, but they offered an abundant supply of attractive material at low prices; and, what was to become increasingly important as automatic machinery became more common, of uniform quality. Although now spoken of as man-made fibres, they were really only man-spun; nature provided the cellulose which was turned into a liquid and then reprecipitated. The next stage in the story starts with such unlikely materials as coal, water, petroleum and limestone, worked upon by a new scientific technique of molecule building.

It was about the year 1925 that the firm of Dupont in America set in train some extremely abstract research on the nature of molecules and for this purpose chose for their studies rubber, silk and cotton. The problem which attracted them was the inadequacy of old theories about the structure of molecules to explain certain properties which were exhibited by some substances, properties which could not be satisfactorily explained by the simple mathematical statement that cellulose, for example, consisted of six atoms of carbon united with ten atoms of hydrogen and five of oxygen. Increasingly refined techniques such, for example, as X-ray analysis indicated that some molecules were complicated aggregates more like complicated cat cradles of chain than simple lumps. It was while they were working on this idea that Dupont's scientists started making compounds which they hoped would prove the truth of their theories, and so it was that by a fortunate accident they found one day that one of their synthetic substances could be drawn out into a fine filament which had great tensile strength, high elasticity and a silk-like appearance. Nylon was born, the first of the family known as synthetic high polymers, the fundamental basis of which is either coal tar or petroleum, from which simple substances such as phenol, glycol and acetylac are obtained. These by complex chemical processes proliferate into more and more complex structures known by such popular names as Nylon, Terylene, Orlon, Courtelle; each one starting from a different base but closely similar in structure.

The chemistry of this story is highly complex and outside our subject, which is the story of the craftsman, and it is from his point of view that we can consider the flood of new substances which poured from the cornucopia of science in the space of little over half a century.

In order to appreciate how violent was the revolution, we must turn back for a moment to the opening chapters which tell the story of how man by painful and slow steps and the method of trial and error evolved fabrics and the tools for making them, but always accepting the fundamental properties of matter as things built into the universe at the Creation.

> Let dogs delight to bark and bite
> It is their nature so to do.

sang the poet, and so to the craftsman the challenge to his skill was the overcoming of the problems arising from the nature of his materials; and, having overcome them, to build up a body of knowledge which was transmitted from one generation to another.

When the new fibres became available, they so closely resembled silk in appearance that it was naturally assumed that the well-established techniques of the silk weaver could be successfully applied to them. But below the superficial resemblance lay fundamental differences and until these were appreciated and, in due course conquered, the weaver might well wonder whether or not the new discoveries were a blessing. There being no such thing as a one-sided medal, the end of the story was a reconciliation of good and bad properties.

By some strange chance the three classic fibres, silk, cotton and wool all behaved in the same way when stretched; provided the tension was kept below the breaking point, they would recover their original length when relaxed; but all the man-made fibres stretch in two ways. In the first phase increasing tension produces stretch which is recovered when the load is taken off; in the second phase the elongation becomes permanent and, just as a steel coil spring can be spoiled if over-stretched, so the filaments of a yarn can be deformed; but with this difference, an over-stretched metal spring is beyond recovery whereas over-stretched yarn recovers its original length either when wetted or heated, and this means that fabric woven from over-stretched threads may pucker or distort in a very unpleasant way when the yarn shrinks.

When the first efforts were made to dye nylon it was found that it had a very low affinity for dyestuffs, partly due to chemical reasons, but also to the fact that whereas cotton or wool when completely wet retain roughly their own weight of water, nylon only retains 25%, in other words wet nylon is dryer than wet cotton or wool, and as dyestuffs are solutions of chemicals it follows that high polymer fibres will be hard to dye; but conversely a thing which is less wet will dry more quickly and so the familiar description 'Drip dry', which is looked on as one of the desirable qualities of the new fibres, is due to what the dyer looks on as a weakness.

Because of the way in which their complex molecules are looped and folded, the high polymer yarns all exhibit characteristic behaviour when heated. In this they resemble steel which can be either annealed or tempered to extreme hardness by heating and cooling.

When nylon or terylene are heated to a certain point the molecules become locked and the fabric will, after it has been distorted, always return to its preset shape. Thus stockings or woven fabric or garments can be given a permanent set so that after becoming creased and folded during washing they will return to their original perfect form. Non-iron garments have a built in tendency to smoothness or rather resist deformation, a quality which is also the basis of 'permanent' pleats or creases.

It is amusing to note that when, by advertising, the public was urged to buy man-made fibre trousers in preference to wool because of their permanent creases, it was not long before scientists found that by suitable chemical treatment wool could also exhibit this desirable property. Necessity may be the mother of invention, but competition is also a powerful spur.

One of the properties for which real silk was esteemed was its warmth combined with lightness, and at first the man-made fibres seemed to lack this. But their ability to accept a predetermined form gave the solution to this difficulty, because what we call warm fabrics owe their property mainly to the air which is entrapped between the fibres rather than to any inherent quality of the material; so if fibres can be made bulky they will automatically feel warm. By twisting and heating the yarn it can be made to assume the form of hollow spirals which are at once warm because of the entrapped air, and elastic because like all spiral forms they stretch under tension. This pleasant combination of qualities, lightness, warmth and stretch have created a great demand for these bulked yarns, and so we have moved forward in a brief half century from a state of affairs where man passively accepted the properties of matter, to one in which, guided by scientific modes of thought, we can become architects with a freedom in design greater than anything known before. The thing to note is the phrase 'scientific modes of thought', which applies not only to original discoveries, but also to methods and processes arising from them.

Fibre Yarns

All over the world there is an abundance of animals and plants having a protective fibrous coat; sheep, goats and camels are typical of the first, and the seed pod of the cotton bush of the second; certain plants such as flax have fibrous structures which can be extracted from their stems.

All these fibres have one feature in common, they are short in length; cotton for example varies from about $\frac{3}{4}$ inch to 2 inches, the others are longer, but such lengths as 6 inches are seldom exceeded. The problem of turning such fibres into long continuous uniform threads is common to all, and is known as spinning. As the threads used in the most ancient specimens of fabric are made either of wool, cotton or linen it is clear that this art is of great antiquity and, like weaving, starting as an exercise in finger dexterity, gradually became mechanised. We have seen in the account of Cartwright's power loom that the sudden abundance of yarn arising from machine spinning was the stimulus to invention.

If we examine a ball of cotton as it comes from the bush,

or wool from the fleece of a sheep, we shall see that they have one feature in common, they consist of a tangled mass of fibres arranged in a random manner and mixed with a good deal of trash. The problem which the craftsman had to solve therefore was threefold; first the fibres had to be arranged in parallel order, secondly the mass of fibres had to be drawn out into a long thin sliver, and thirdly the fibres had to be bound together to form a strong smooth uniform thread capable of withstanding the strain of weaving.

We all know that human hair, if left to its own devices, becomes a tangled mass which can be brought to order by brushing and combing, and it is by these two processes that fibres are brought into parallel order. If we then pull at the two ends of the parallel bunch of fibres, we shall find that it does not at once come apart but stretches to a considerable length just as a telescope extends when pulled. If we then twist the ends of the bunch of fibres between the finger and thumb, it will shrink in diameter and become compacted into a thread which when released will retain its form and will have acquired a surprising degree of strength. The question naturally arises—where does this strength come from? Why do fibres stick together?

The microscope provides the answer. It shows that in the case of cotton the fibres are not circular but flat and naturally twisted, rather like barley sugar, while wool fibres are covered with minute scales rather like those of a fish. When, therefore, two fibres touch one another the spirals or scales interlock and it is this interlocking which gives the strength. So the spinning process does two things; it makes the thread more compact and fine and it increases the interlocking whereby the strength is also increased.

Anyone who goes for a country walk may find a tuft of wool on a hedge and with the aid of a stiff bristled tooth brush and a good deal of patience may, after a number of failures, spin a few inches of rather lumpy thread made up of a few hundred fibres. After which instructive exercise he may then dissect such a fabric as a fine handerkerchief or a bit of fine wool cloth and, realising that in a square yard are many millions of fibres, each so fine that they are just visible to the naked eye, will begin to appreciate the exquisite skill of the spinner and the delicacy of the machinery which had to be evolved when spinning became an automatic process.

The whole mystery of spinning can be studied with the aid of a reel of sewing cotton and a wooden skewer to form a spindle and by varying the angle at which the thread winds on or off. If the bobbin is rotated and the thread is fed on at right angles to the spindle, then winding or unwinding without change of form takes place; if, however, we catch the thread in the small nick found in the flange of the bobbin and carry the thread so that it is in line with the axis of the spindle then, when the spindle is rotated, twist will be put in the yarn which will grow tighter and tighter until the thread breaks under the strain. Any device, therefore, which will spin yarn must combine these two motions. This may be done in two ways; either we may alternate the processes of twisting and winding up, in which case we have invented the distaff and hand spinning wheel that eventually developed into the mule; or we can combine the two so that they are going on simultaneously and so evolve what is known as ring spinning.

In hand spinning the worker alternates the two types of rotation and controls the tension by his fingers; the spindle either being twirled between finger and thumb or turned by a wheel. The neolithic spindle whorls made from baked clay or pierced stones were really the flywheels or spinning-tops which kept the earliest spindles in rotation, the fineness and uniformity of the thread being entirely dependent on the accuracy with which the worker drew the fibres from the unspun mass. For thousands of years, therefore, the spinning of thread involved immense labour, one pair of hands being necessary for the production of a single thread. As in playing the violin, touch was everything, and it was not until after the year 1700 that machines were evolved for performing these operations automatically.

The first invention was made in 1738 by Lewis Paul, who realised that if the roving or bunch of parallel fibres was passed between two sets of rollers, the second revolving faster than the first, they would become attenuated. His own description, given in his patent specification is very clear, he says, 'The wool or cotton being thus prepared, one end of the mass, Rope thread or sliver is put betwixt a pair of rowlers, cillinders or cones, or some such movements, which being twined round by their motion draws in the raw mass of wool or cotton to be spun in proportion to the velocity of such rowlers cillinders or cones: as the prepared mass passes regularly through or betwixt these rowlers, cillinders or cones a succession of other Rowlers cillinders or cones moveing proportionably faster than the first, draw the rope thread or sliver into any degree of fineness which may be required.'

This establishes beyond a doubt that Paul was the inventor of drafting or attenuation of fibres.

Mechanically refined and improved, Paul's invention is still used today as the first stage in spinning even in the most up-to-date mills.

The next inventor was Hargreaves, who in 1768 solved the problem of operating a large number of spindles simultaneously by mounting them in a frame, each being driven by a belt from a revolving drum. A corresponding number of supply bobbins furnished the yarn, which was drawn off and fixed by a pair of clamping bars. The essence of the machine was the faller wire or guide which in one position presented the thread to the tip of the spindle, and in the other to its circumference. When, by the turning of a hand wheel, the spindles were rotated the yarn was twisted, after which the faller moved to the winding-on position, and the clamping bars having been released, the yarn was wound up and a fresh supply drawn into the machine; by moving the clamping bar backwards after it was closed, the drawing out of the threads was achieved. The machine therefore was an intermittent draw frame, twister and winder.

All over the country inventors were working on these problems and about 1786 Arkwright invented the Throstle Frame, so called because when at work it made a whistling sound reminiscent of a thrush singing. He adopted Paul's roller system of drafting and after the last pair of rollers fed the untwisted fibre through a flyer onto the spinning bobbin, so combining twisting and winding-up in one operation. This is the principle on which modern ring spinning works; but in its early days this method had one weakness, the twist was fixed into the yarn at the point when it left the feed roller and so any slight variation was fixed as a thick or thin place, whereas in Hargreave's Jenny, irregularities tended to even themselves out over the whole length of yarn drawn out.

While therefore it is true that Hargreaves was the originator of the spinning jenny, economic factors and other people were involved; and, contrary to popular belief, the mule did not immediately supersede the jenny, which, radically improved by many inventors, continued to be in wide use well into the 19th century.

It is only within the last few years that Industrial Archaeology has become a serious study and we are indebted to Mr. C. Aspin and Mr. S. D. Chapman for a careful piece of research into the Hargreaves story (published by the Helmshore Local History Society under the title *James Hargreaves and the Spinning Jenny*).

Not only have they consulted contemporary letters and newspapers, but helped by a skilled woodworker Mr. D. Pilkington and the firm of Textile Machinery Makers (Research) Ltd., have actually constructed a working model as specified in the descriptions or drawings of Hargreaves' original patent. Skilled spinners then helped by operating the machine on a range of cotton yarns and so a critical evaluation of his work could be made (Plate 19).

From this research a number of interesting facts have been established and the following summary gives an outline of the true story. The Helmshore jenny when built closely resembled a hand spinning wheel tipped over on its side, thus confirming the story that the accidental overturning of a wheel which continued to revolve and spin gave Hargreaves his first inspiration; but the development of the idea owed a great deal to the efforts of Robert Peel, grandfather of Sir Robert Peel. In its early form the jenny was essentially a cottage machine having only 16 spindles. The early accounts speak of the machine as being better adapted for use by children, and this is found to be true when one studies the position of the driving wheel, which was so low that an adult would suffer from backache when working it. The careful spinning experiments show that Hargreaves had only solved the problems of spinning coarse counts of cotton weft; firm warp yarns were technically beyond the scope of the jenny and a number of mechanical improvements had to be made before it could handle wool. With these improvements plus the building of much larger machines, jenny spinning became a factory process and, because they were cheap to install and easy to build, they continued to compete successfully with the more costly mule. It was these larger and more elaborate machines which spread across into Yorkshire, where they were widely used in the woollen trade well into the 19th century. These spinning tests also confirm the truth of the story that it was his complete failure to spin fine warp yarn on a jenny which stimulated Crompton to work on his invention of the mule.

Mr. Aspin and Mr. Chapman have not only produced a book which is interesting for its own sake but one which shows the need for more scholarly work on the story of the early history of the Industrial Revolution. Modern technology has made us so familiar today with the scientific approach to development, that we tend to ignore the period in which flashes of inspired genius and the labours of skilled craftsmen in wood and iron, stimulated by imaginative business men such as Peel, combined to produce results which in a single century revolutionised man's productive resources. It was Crompton who by 1779 had perfected a machine which combined ideas from Arkwright and Hargreaves and, because of its hybrid origin, became known as the mule. As designed by Crompton the cycle of operations was manually controlled and it was not till 1830 that Roberts made the whole machine automatic. For spinning yarn of the most superb quality and fineness the mule proved to be the most perfect instrument, and although for economic reasons and also because of the gradual elimination of its mechanical weaknesses the ring frame has now become the most popular machine, the mule was the foundation on which the prosperity and technical supremacy of the British textile industry was built up during the 19th century.

Most of us were taught at school that the cotton industry flourished in Lancashire because of the moist climate. This was indeed a factor but tends to give the impression that the whole matter was like the abundance of rabbits in Australia or blackberries in New Zealand and so fails to pay proper tribute to the amazing skill of the craftsmen both in textiles and in engineering. These men, without the engineering resources and technological skills we enjoy today, solved not only in principle but, at a high level of perfection, the problems of what we today speak of as automation.

Plate 20 shows a mule in operation. This gives a vivid picture of the growth in productivity, which took place in less than a century, when we compare it with the picture of a native woman spinning a single strand.

The cycle of operations can be divided into three phases: in phase one the carriage which carries the spindles rolls forward drawing out about a yard and a half of yarn; in phase two the faller wires move the thread to the tip of the spindles which then rotate a predetermined number of times until exactly the required twist has been put in; in phase three the faller wires change to the winding position, and as the carriage rolls back the yarn which has been spun is gathered up.

When it is realised that yarns so fine that 100,000 yards only weighing a pound were commonly spun on this machine, it will be seen how delicately it must have been made. Today electronic devices make it easy to control machines which perform a cyclical series of operations, but a century and a half ago such things did not exist and so the cam was the brain and memory of the machine.

The art of spinning fibres seems to have arisen all over the world as soon as men abandoned the nomadic way of life and began to live in settled communities, and the raw materials chosen depended mainly on geography soil and climate. Basic techniques were the same but had to be modified in accordance with the properties of the material.

Many plants and animals furnished the weaver with his raw materials, but a few have by their natural abundance been at all

F

times the most common. The following notes give a brief account of these.

Cotton

Among plants of the mallow family is the *Genus gossipium* or cotton bush, a shrubby plant whose seed pods when ripe burst and reveal a mass of fine hairs, called a boll, varying in colour from white or pale brown and in length from ⅔ inch to 2 inches. For its profitable cultivation cotton must have a fertile soil and a climate following the pattern of abundant spring rain, a hot summer with some light rain, and finally a dry warm autumn, in order to ensure the ripening and harvesting of the crop. It is also a plant calling for clean cultivation and, in spite of many attempts at mechanisation, a large cheap labour force for the picking of the bolls. Geographically these conditions are found between the latitudes 43° N. and 33° S. and, provided the soil is suitable, cotton growing can only flourish where there is an abundant supply of low-paid labour; the availability of slaves in the Southern States of the U.S.A. and peasants in Egypt and India were the reason for these areas being the principal sources of supply.

The choicest quality of cotton comes from the West Indies and the Gulf of Florida; the fibres are exceptionally long and fine and it is these two properties which control the fineness of the yarns which can be spun. Known to the trade as Sea Island cotton, this choice and costly material has a natural beauty for looks and durability. Such fabrics as lawn and voile and the highest grades of shirtings are made from Sea Island yarn.

Much greater in quantity and next in quality comes Egyptian cotton, fine in texture it has a long staple and so can be spun in fine counts. The drawback of a naturally dry climate is overcome by irrigation from the Nile. A great deal of research has gone into the breeding and improved cultivation of this cotton and it is in such world-wide demand that it forms a major part of the Egyptian economy.

The most abundant production of cotton comes from the Southern States of the U.S.A., and is known as American Upland.

Strong and of medium fibre length, this is the great bread and butter cotton of the world and the fact that the Southern States of America were ideal for its growth together with the use of slave labour caused cotton to play an important role in American history.

Finally we have Indian cotton, short in staple and produced by a species of bush having a deep root system which enables it to resist drought conditions; this, although of low quality, is a major part of the world supply.

As nature evolved cotton fibre for the protection of the seeds of the Gossipium species and not in order to provide man with raw material, the boll contains less than half its own weight of cotton, hence the crop as harvested is bulky and contains only a small proportion of useful material; so it is that the first two processes of manufacture are carried out on the farms. It was Eli Whitney who in 1792 invented the machine called a gin, whereby the fibres could be detached from the seeds. It consists of a revolving cylinder with teeth like those of a circular saw, which tear the fibres from the mass, leaving the seeds behind; powerful presses then reduce the material in bulk and it then consists of compressed bolls which are sent to the factories for further treatment. Firmly attached to the seed is an inner coating of hairs too short to be spun; these are removed separately and sold as cotton linters—an important source of raw material for the manufacture of rayon.

Despite its ancient history in India, Peru and Egypt, cotton was not known in Europe till Magellan found the Brazilians using vegetable down. Cortes sent samples of cotton cloth from Mexico to Spain and even as late as 1664 we find Samuel Pepys involved in a dispute about whether calico was or was not linen for import tax purposes. 'They say it is made of cotton wool and grows on trees,' he reported. Throughout history one definition of a foreigner has been 'An ill paid rascal who by his cheap and inferior goods takes the bread from the mouths of honest Englishmen'. Thus in the early 18th century the wool industry protested against the importing of cotton; it was not till 1774 that Parliament passed a law sanctioning the manufacture of cotton goods subject to a duty of 3d per yard, and that the goods were stamped with a seal for the counterfeiting of which the penalty was hanging. It may be true that history never repeats itself, but it is interesting to note than in Australia, where there is so great a vested interest in wool, the same animosity towards man-made fibres has been shown, although of course the more humane Australians have never included the death penalty as part of their trade legislation.

Wool

As early as 9000 B.C. men had begun to domesticate the sheep which existed in a wild state both in Europe and Asia. Probably first used as a source of food and skin, the sheep's wool was soon found to be useful as a spinning fibre and the oldest textile fabric in the world was made (*circa* 6500 B.C.) from this raw material. Tough and hardy and able to exist on the sparse herbage of mountainous country or drought areas, and able to survive semi-arctic cold or Australian heat, together with the fortunate accident that the wool fibres have a natural power of cohesion due to microscopic scales on their surface, the sheep has been the source of the commonest textile raw material. That wool fibres in the case of shorn sheep are from 2 to 16 inches long makes for ease of spinning and of course the outstanding property of wool is its warmth which is due to the air trapped between the fibres. A remarkable property of wool is its natural tendency to felting, that is to say, when it is beaten in the presence of moisture, the fibres become more and more compacted. This is the basis of a number of finishing processes used on wool cloth, whereby the original grain of the weave as it comes from the loom is changed into a close, firm material. One of the most interesting examples of a highly finished wool fabric is billiard table cloth, which has been subjected to such a degree of finishing as to lose completely its original structure. On the other hand the great length of the wool fibre means that the ends can be teased out and made fluffy without becoming detached from the main structure of the thread, and so it is by brushing that blankets are given their good heat insulating qualities combined with extreme lightness.

Selective breeding has produced many types of sheep, each of which gives wool of a characteristic quality, some being fine and lustrous while others are tough and wiry; the latter is suitable for the weaving of carpets in which the resiliency of the pile causes it to recover from being trodden down, while at the same time resisting the friction of treading.

Finally we must note a property which wool shares only with silk in being the base on which the dyer can exercise his skill with the greatest freedom; namely its natural affinity for the whole gamut of colours which, together with its combination of density with lustre, gives the craftsman a scope for freedom of fancy not yet equalled by any of the synthetic fibres. It seems a pity therefore that the sheep from which we enjoy so many benefits has become synonymous with stupidity and, as Handel noted, has a tendency to stray.

Vicuna

Living high up on the bleak mountain slopes of Chile and Peru and therefore needing protection from almost arctic cold, there are herds of animals of the llama family known as vicuna of which the coat, although technically a wool, is so fine and silky that it is justifiably classified by itself. When spun and woven it produces cloth which is exceptionally light and warm and pleasant both to the eye and to touch. Owing to its scarcity it commands very high prices.

Cashmere

Regrettably used all too often as an adjective descriptive of other fibres having soft silky appearance, the word cashmere is a noun and applies to the fleece of the cashmere goat of Northern India. It is one of the most beautiful fibres and is, today, best known as the material used for knitted garments but for the weaver it is the basis of the famous Paisley shawls. These were originally woven in India on simple hand looms but were reproduced in Paisley. The revival of interest in Victorian designs may direct attention to what were masterpieces of fine weaving of beautiful material.

Alpaca

Whereas the vicuna is a wild animal, the alpaca has long been domesticated, and great herds of these animals which have the body of a sheep with a neck like a camel, are kept by the South American Indians on the mountain slopes of Chile, Peru and Bolivia. Living at a height of 14,000 feet above sea-level they develop a fine dense coat which is shorn at regular intervals.

Introduced into Europe by the early explorers who sent home samples of the yarn and also specimens of cloth woven by the native Peruvians, alpaca made little or no progress. At first its properties made it too difficult to spin and it was not until 1836 that Sir Titus Salt by the application of very ingenious methods solved the problem. This remarkable man founded his fortune by another piece of inventiveness, the spinning of a peculiar type of Russian wool called donskoi, but his great discovery was the technique of spinning alpaca. His success was enormous and a great industry grew up in the Bradford area. He was a man with ideas far ahead of his age. He built the model town of Saltaire where he put into practice ideas on housing, town planning and industrial relationships far ahead of anything previously thought of. He is the supreme example of a craftsman whose ingenuity founded a fortune which, because of his liberal and humane ideas, became the mainspring of one of the earliest essays in what we now call the social sciences.

Naturally black or dark brown in colour, alpaca has a curious silky crispness and was immensely popular in Victorian days as a dress material. It is nowadays mainly used for linings and men's light-weight jackets; but in its heyday a black alpaca dress was an essential item in the wardrobe of a Victorian matriarch.

Camel Hair

One of the writers on the camel said, 'He is from first to last an undomesticated and savage animal rendered serviceable by stupidity alone, without much skill on his master's part or any co-operation on his own'. Nevertheless he furnishes the weaver with a useful material which has two strangely contrasted properties. The finer fibres, naturally tawny in colour, make a delightfully soft and pleasant cloth, although it should be pointed out that much of the beauty of a camel-hair coat is due rather to the art of the cloth finisher than to the weave employed.

The large and coarser fibres are of great mechanical strength and for many years camel hair belting was greatly esteemed by engineers for its durability and gripping power.

Linen

It is a debatable question whether the first neolithic weavers used linen or wool as their raw material, but as the earliest use of thread may well have been for sewing skins together or for lashing wood and cane together or for binding stone tools to wooden handles, the immense strength of linen thread may have made it the first textile to be spun.

The flax plant is a hardy annual from the stems of which long tough lustrous fibres can be extracted by a fermentation process known as retting. Pliny in his *Natural History* gives a clear account of how the stems were put into tanks of water and held down by stones. Even today wherever flax is cultivated this noxious process is the first stage of manufacture, followed by hacking or tearing with strong metal combs; thereafter the processes of spinning are in principle similar to those used for wool or cotton.

In ancient times linen was highly esteemed; Pharaoh arrayed Joseph in 'Vestures of fine linen', and the importance of the flax crop to the Egyptians is shown by the destruction caused by the plague of hail, 'the barley was in the ear and the flax was bolled' (Exodus, IX, 31). Priestly garments were of linen and mummies were wrapped in linen cloth.

Unfortunately the processes of growing flax and preparing linen are intensely laborious, so that in spite of its superb quality as a fibre it has declined in importance, first by the competition of cotton and later by that of man-made fibres.

Spun Synthetic Yarns

Having with great skill solved the problem of making a viscous fluid and extruding it so as to simulate the silkworm's thread, men promptly turned their attention to the second question—was it possible to chop the filaments into short lengths and then to spin them by either the cotton or wool system into a thread which would resemble those yarns?

This at first sight may remind us of Miss Anna Russell's ladies' club which one month had a lecture on how to make patchwork quilts out of old dresses, and the next month a lecture on how to make dresses out of old patchwork quilts; but the matter was not as paradoxical as would appear at first sight.

Filament yarns are shiny and translucent, slippery and not very warm and so from the weaver's point of view can only be used for a limited range of fabrics; also the rising cost of natural fibres offered a tempting bait to ingenuity; and so a large range of cotton and wool substitutes was evolved. In the early days much was heard of 'The Battle of the Fibres' but common sense soon showed that blended materials often gave more pleasing results at reasonable cost than a pure fibre.

Known by proprietary trade names such as Fibro, Courtelle, Orlon, these materials are triumphs of chemistry allied to textile skill and presented the craftsman with problems which were not quickly overcome. The spinner, the dyer and the weaver each had to modify his traditional skill in order to overcome the difficulties of manipulating the new materials, but as in most cases it was a question of modification rather than new invention the subject is rather outside the scope of this book; but one property which all the new materials showed was a strong tendency to generate static electricity which causes the fibres to 'stand on end like the quills upon the fretful porpentine'. A machine using nylon can become so powerfully charged with electricity as to give unpleasant shocks to the worker unless it is earthed; so a great deal of research has gone into anti-static chemicals for application to the yarn or apparatus for neutralising the electric charge by bombardment with electrons of the opposite character. It is not only in politics that we have to 'Bring in the new world to redress the balance of the old'; hence the technologist is a man who, in order to practice his own art successfully must become learned in all the sciences.

The Battle of the Fibres

During the past fifty years highly interested parties have spilt a good deal of ink on what is rather a Tweedledum, Tweedledee conflict; and as in all propaganda, passion obscures and distorts truth. To the weaver all fibres are just raw materials, each having its own good and bad points and so like Mercutio he can say, 'A plague o' both your houses!'

The following notes are therefore intended to set out impartially the pros and cons of the matter.

Contrary to the fears of those whose livelihood rested on the great natural fibres such as silk, wool and cotton, the man-made fibres have not had any serious effect for two reasons. First because world fibres consumption has, with expanding population, grown so greatly that the new materials have found their own place, and secondly, the demand for land needed to produce food has become so great that farmers have tended to concentrate on the main profitable activity.

Nowhere is this more evident than in Japan where farmers have scrapped their mulberry trees and so have abandoned the laborious rearing of silkworms in favour of food production.

Apart from its other attractions, viscose rayon has the virtue that its basic raw material, wood-pulp, is produced from trees which flourish on poor soils.

The high polymer fibres such as Nylon, Terylene, Orlon and Courtelle are all fruits of the petro-chemical tree and as far as we can see will tend to become cheaper and more abundant in the oil and natural gas era in which we now live. Unlike natural products, the crop of which fluctuates widely with weather changes and the incidence of disease, the synthetics are very stable in price.

Three properties which make the new synthetics attractive are linked with changes in fashion and social habits which have come about in recent years.

The first is their low water absorption characteristic which makes them 'drip dry'; cotton and wool even when heavily mangled retain their own weight of water and therefore dry slowly after washing whereas the synthetics can only absorb a quarter of their own weight. Secondly they are thermoplastic which means that by heat treatment after weaving, the cloth can be given a permanent set so that pleats and creases once put in are not affected by washing and conversely flatness is permanent. So 'minimum iron' is now a familiar sales slogan.

Thirdly there is the extreme fineness to which they can be spun, thus making for very light-weight inexpensive fabrics. As one economist has put it:

> In the reign of Queen Victoria it took two sheep to clothe a woman; now, one silkworm scarcely has to work full time.

Although by these properties the new fibres have made a powerful challenge to the traditional ones, it is still true however that for fineness and beauty silk remains the 'Queen of Fibres', while for warmth, durability and pleasant appearance wool is so far supreme, and for cheapness and hard wearing combined with much beauty cotton is still the most widely used fibre in the world.

As so often happens the end of the battle of the fibres is a compromise, and today an ever increasing use is made of mixture yarns when the spinner combines natural and synthetic fibres to make the best use of all their properties.

Yarn Counts

Vague words such as fine or coarse are useless, we must have standards, especially if the question of value is to come into our calculations.

When the new sciences were born it was realised that international standards were essential, and so the volt, ampère and ohm were adopted from the beginning; but in the case of textiles, the roots of which go so far back that contact between people in adjacent valleys was negligible, local systems were evolved, each logical in itself but showing a fine disregard for other places and other fibres. If we put back the clock and try to study the problem as it must have appeared to the first weavers we shall appreciate the difficulties. Diameter is ruled out as a basis of measurement for two reasons, first because the threads are so fine that micrometers measuring in thousandths of an inch would be necessary, and secondly, even if we had them, the soft and compressible nature of yarn makes diameter extremely difficult to measure accurately.

What we can do is either to take standard lengths of yarn and weigh them or standard weights of yarn and measure how many yards they contain; each gives an intelligent answer.

In the case of silk the first method was chosen, and so the denier number is the weight in grams of 9,000 metres, whereas in cotton standard skeins, each of 840 yards, were put in a scale till a weight of 1 lb. was reached. The number of skeins is then the count number of the yarn. Because Lancashire men and Yorkshire men never see eye to eye the worsted spinners opted for a 560 yard skein. Therefore we have two quite dissimilar scales; in the case of silk and man-made fibres the denier number rises as the yarn gets thicker, whereas in the case of cotton and wool low numbers mean coarse, and high numbers fine yarn.

To add to the confusion, different practices were adopted when several strands were first spun and afterwards folded together. In the case of cotton and wool the expression 60/2 means that two threads of 60s count have been twisted together to make a final thread which is equal to 30/1, but when real silk waste is spun and folded the number 60 is the resultant count and 60/2 means that two threads each 120 count have been twisted together.

No logical justification can be offered for this confusion and many valiant, but unsuccessful, attempts have been made to establish a universal count system; but for the time being just as Frenchmen and Greeks show a rigid preference for their native language so the various branches of the textile trade cling to their own systems.

CHAPTER FIVE

Dyeing and Finishing

IF the weaver depended only on his own skill the products of his loom would be drab in colour and often unpleasing to the touch; only by making use of the services of the dyer and finisher is his work brought to full beauty.

This is a difficult subject on which to write briefly because it stretches, in time, from ancient Egypt and India when the first discoveries were made, right through to the 20th century when some of the most advanced chemical discoveries have been made in the production of new dyes; and also because we touch on the subject of aesthetics, where subjective judgements are involved and these are not measurable; 'Clothed in purple and fine linen' or 'Shocking' pink are both expressions of the dyer's art and such descriptions as 'Suede or Doeskin' finish are allied to the work of the biblical fuller.

In *Twelfth Night* Shakespeare says, '. . . the tailor make thy doublet of changeable taffeta, for thy mind is a very opal', showing that he was familiar with the effect which the dyer could have on a plain cloth, by dyeing warp and weft in strongly contrasting colours. Today changeable taffeta is known as shot silk.

A barbed shaft of wit is described as mordant, a term borrowed from the dyer, who even in ancient times found that certain substances would cause dyes to bite more keenly on to the fibre. And Polly Peacham ('The Beggar's Opera) says, 'Money is the true fuller's earth for reputations, there's not a spot or stain but what it can take out'. Although no longer used, fuller's earth was for centuries the best grease remover.

In the Middle Ages Coventry true blue was universally admired for its purity and fastness, and cloth dyed by this method commanded high prices.

Ancient specimens of cloth from many parts of the world show that, in early times, men had discovered a number of natural substances which would stain textile materials. Indigo was used in Thebes as early as 3000 B.C.; plants such as saffron gave yellow shades, whilst a sea snail (Murex) was the source of the Tyrian or royal purple. Archil, a colour produced by the action of ammonia derived from stale urine on certain lichens, was known to Pliny. Weaving and dyeing therefore developed side by side as allied arts.

The discovery of America brought to Europe new substances which had long been used by the Mexicans and Peruvians and so increased the dyer's resources; logwood for black and cochineal for scarlet were among these. The developing and fixing of colours by mordants was known in India about 2000 B.C.

The range of natural colours was limited and it was not until the 19th century that chemists, by the discovery of coal tar derivatives, opened up the treasure house of dyestuffs which are, today, the basis of modern dyeing.

The father of modern dyeing was Sir William Henry Perkin (1838–1907), who, while seeking to make artificial quinine, treated aniline with bichromate of potash and obtained a black substance from which he extracted a bluish one, which became known as Aniline Purple or Mauve. Today, this dye is only of historic interest, but its discovery was a landmark in the history of dyeing and, once Perkin had shown the way, it was not long before others followed. Before the end of the century a complete range of synthetic colours had been evolved, many of them reaching a standard of fastness to light and to washing much exceeding that of natural dyestuffs.

Since the turn of the century the petroleum industry has added many new chemicals to the range; and from these other types of dyestuffs have been evolved. Much of the research was stimulated by the peculiarities of some of the new man-made fibres; acetate rayon, for example, seemed at first to have no affinity for dyes and a new range of colours had to be evolved; Nylon and Terylene have presented similar problems.

In the Middle Ages, dyes were classified as 'Noble and Lesser

Dyes' and heavy penalties were imposed on those who practiced fraud in this matter. In order to qualify for the distinction of being called Noble, a dye had to be resistant to fading and washing.

Today, the laundry and the domestic washing machine, both of which may involve the use of strong chemicals, and the habit of sun bathing and swimming in heavily chlorinated water, have introduced new and more searching tests than the old dyers ever knew.

Not only must a good dye be inherently fast, but it must be well applied; the false economy of using strong solutions in order to shorten the working time is a temptation which has to be resisted, as is that of 'topping'. The means that, having reached almost the correct shade, the final stage is arrived at by a rinse in a fugitive dye, which in use will wash off or fade, but for the moment will give pleasure to the eye. Anyone who takes a walk round a modern store or who examines the textiles in their home will be impressed with the variety and quality of modern dye techniques but as one distinguished dyer said, 'Dyeing may be a branch of science but it is still remarkably like tuning a violin'.

First of all there must be not only optical, but also chemical cleanliness of the yarn. Wool contains grease, and cotton has a natural wax, and both contain natural colouring substances which if left alone would make the dye colour dingy. Prolonged scouring and bleaching are therefore the pre-treatment for dyeing; and these also remove grease and oil stains due to manufacturing processes. Then comes the preparation of the dye liquor itself, involving water which must be pure to standards more strict than those which apply to domestic purposes; and finally, the selection and blending of the dyes and this plural term should be carefully noted because the dye mixer, despite all the scientific aids now at his command is still the master craftsman in a dyeworks.

The first thing to remember is that very few dyestuffs used as pure colour are artistically pleasing, and therefore blending is essential. This means mixing two or three substances together.

Here is where the difficulties begin, because dyestuffs not only differ in hue, but also in their behaviour: some are more or less active according to temperature; others behave differently with the passage of time, that is to say a dye having what is called a powerful strike will develop the full colour in a minute or two while others build up slowly; some act uniformly from start to finish while others start by producing a patchy effect which gradually levels out after the lapse of time. With so many variables the task of the dyer can be likened to that of a driver of a team of horses one of which dashes off at a gallop, one trots steadily while the third wants a crack of the whip to get it moving.

So sensitive is the human eye to slight variations of tone and hue that all this has to be controlled to standards of fineness which involve measurements of dye concentration expressed in fractions of one per cent; a minute trace of the correct yellow will change a crude shade of candy pink to an exotic peach colour. The feminine eye is exceptionally aware of subtle differences and in the corsetry and lingerie trades there are normally about thirty shades which can all be described as tea rose, blush or peach; a number which is increased when an old colour is, for reasons of *haute couture*, rechristened with some exotic new name.

To enumerate all the different types of dye and to describe in detail their appropriate techniques would be wearisome, but one or two points of general interest are worth special mention.

Vat dyeing. This does not imply the use of vats, the name signifies outstanding fastness of colour, which arises from the method of application in two stages. The first is an impregnation with a liquor that deposits reagent 'A' in the fibres, an after-treatment with reagent 'B' causes a reaction within the molecular structure of the fibre and generates the final dye substance, which is insoluble and consists of molecules of considerable size. By generating the dye within the threads exceptional fastness is obtained.

Pigment Dyeing. Early in the history of Rayon the idea of impregnating the viscose with colouring matter was mastered, but the practical difficulties were very great and so it is only since the war that a range of pre-pigmented yarns has become available. Combining cheapness with a high degree of fastness, it has given the weaver new technical resources of great potential value.

Mercerising. This is not really a dye process, although it is carried out by dyers; it is a means of adding increased lustre to cotton; which, if the raw material is of high quality, may be given a lustre comparable to that of real silk. The process is named after John Mercer who, in 1843 was experimenting with caustic soda as a means of increasing the bulkiness of cotton yarns. If this treatment is carried out in a tank, no change in lustre is noted but if the material is treated under tension then the surface change takes place. Not only is the appearance enhanced but the dyeing affinity of the cellulose is improved.

Fabric Dyeing and Finishing

Only a small proportion of all the cloth which is woven reaches the user in loom state; for this there are two reasons. It is cheaper to weave in bulk and dye afterwards rather than to dye small quantities of warp and weft separately, and also because the appeal both to hand and eye are qualities which depend on the finisher rather than the weaver. Moreover the twisting and weaving of the threads create strains and stresses in the fabric which, unless controlled, show up as shrinkage and cockling.

So far as dyeing is concerned, the methods and materials used are the same as for yarn. The cloth, after scouring, is either passed through the dye liquor or the dye is pumped under pressure through the material. In the case of very delicate materials the fabric is hung from hooks attached to a star frame so that it is coiled in an open spiral—if we imagine a long curtain hanging from a rail which has been formed into a spiral shape, we get a picture of what is done (see Figure 16). The whole mass is then lowered into a circular vat in which the dye is circulated. The result of all this is to produce colour but the effect on the fabric is to leave it utterly limp and lustreless, like washing when it comes from a spin-dryer. In the case of satins, the high gloss is restored by the use of hot high pressure mangles, but for taffetas and crêpes this would be fatal and so they are finished on a stenter;

Figure 16. The Star Frame

which is, in principle, a long oven through which the cloth is carried by being attached to small hooks fixed on two parallel endless belts placed far enough apart to stretch the cloth back to its original width.

The popular phrase, 'To be on tenterhooks' is a vivid word picture of the state of affairs inside a stenter. Control of tension at the feed point gives warpwise stretch and hot air or radiant, heat fix the cloth in flat form.

When the natural rigidity of the fibre is not sufficient, additional stiffness was formerly added by starch, but this is a fugitive effect and so today synthetic resins, which are water resistant, are used. The popular crease resistant finishes are produced in this way.

In the case of wool, much more elaborate finishing processes are involved and these are possible because wool is by nature thermo plastic, i.e. it behaves like human hair, which when heated in the presence of moisture, assumes a permanent wave. If we compare a Donegal tweed, which is almost a loom state cloth,

G

with a fine West of England suiting, and remember that at the moment of weaving they are remarkably alike, we shall realise how much of the final effect is due to the finisher's art. Steaming, beetling (beating with heavy, wooden hammers) brushing to raise a pile, which is then shaved off by cropping with rotary knives, are all stages along the road from weaver to wearer.

A well-made suit is therefore a successful partnership between three craftsmen, the weaver, who •by good yarn selection and fabric structure lays the foundation, the finisher who enhances and reveals the inherent beauty of the cloth, and the tailor, who builds the final shape.

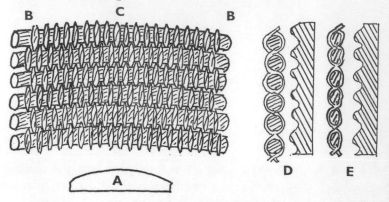

Figure 17. The basis of moiré finish

One process used in fabric finishing has about it an air of mystery—the moiré or water wave effect—especially as no water is employed in the process. It is an ingenious optical illusion.

If we study Figure 17 the underlying principle will be understood. On the right at D and E we see a ribbed fabric being pressed against the teeth of a metal rack. If, as at D, ridges in the one correspond to hollows in the other, no effect will be produced; but if, as at E, ridge meets ridge, then the soft fabric will be crushed and deformed.

This is the basis of moiré finish, which can only be applied to boldly ribbed fabric woven from silk, cotton or filament rayon, i.e. yarn having a naturally high lustre. The rack shown at D and E is replaced by a heated metal roller in which fine teeth have been cut. These, in theory, should exactly mesh with the ribs of the cloth. If we now distort the ribs by dragging the cloth over a scraper A we shall get conformity at BB and non-conformity at C or the converse and, because the cloth is elastic, the effect will be random. Where the ribs are uncrushed and retain their cylindrical form they will look dark; but where they have been flattened, a highlight will be created, and this will look pale. As the ribs are small and the light and dark areas merge into one another the eye perceives a total effect which resembles the grain pattern seen in certain types of wood, notably pitch pine.

Designing in Colour

In the first chapter, we traced the evolution of decorative weaving from simple twills up to the brocade fabric, which is the last word in elaborate ornamentation, blending form and colour at the wish of the artist; but, as in all things, there is a drawback. Each additional colour means an extra weft, thus increasing the weight and stiffness of the cloth. Hangings and upholstery for lofty rooms and ecclesiastical vestments are not affected by this limitation, but the modern desire for light-weight fabrics means that, if decoration is to be achieved, then we must solve the problem of weightless colours, and it is here that dyeing and its allied art of fabric printing play their part.

No sooner had the dyer learned to produce plain coloured cloth than he sought to make patterns by local application of dye. One of the earliest methods, and one which any amateur may practise for amusement, is to take a square of white cloth which has been well washed and dried and scatter small pebbles over the surface. Holding each pebble from the back, i.e. through the cloth, a tight ligature is bound in such a way as to trap the pebbles in little mushroom-shaped bags. The whole piece is then dyed and dried and the ligatures cut. The result is a pattern of roughly circular shapes, rather like aster flowers. Diluted red ink or strong black coffee may serve as the dye.

Like all patterns made by mechanical means, the method is of limited value because the shapes tend to become monotonous.

The problem of giving the artist his freedom to design at will was solved long ago in Java, where the art of Batik dyeing was discovered and brought to an amazing standard of perfection. In theory the process is very simple; but in practice it calls for the highest degree of skill.   In batik there is no rubbing out.   After elaborate washing and softening, the cloth is stretched out and the design is drawn on by means of hot wax, or in lacquer, known as the resit, forming the negative of the pattern desired; that is to say, those parts which are to show the ground colour are waxed over leaving the others free to absorb dye.   The wax is put on from small pots, each fitted with a delicate spout, their diameter and shape controlling the thickness of the line which is drawn. Such is the skill of the workers, that lines as fine as those produced by an artist who draws in Indian ink, can be produced, and so the most delicate forms of flowers and insects can be made.   In some cases the design is sketched in with charcoal before the waxing takes place but some workers are so skilled and confident that they draw straight in with the wax pot or *tjanting*.

When the wax has set the cloth is dyed with the first colour and then de-waxed.   Successive waxings and dyeings gradually build up the final pattern.   In Java the patterns were traditional and museums have specimens showing how they were kept over long periods without change.

Since the Dutch introduced Batik to Europe the scope and flexibility have attracted the attention of artists, who have found pleasure in working in this medium; but as it is a hand process, there has been no development on a commercial scale.

The earliest European printing on fabric was done by using engraved wooden blocks, exactly like those used by book printers. These, after being spread with the colour stiffened to a creamy paste, are struck with a wooden mallet.   The effects which can be produced are of great delicacy and, for choice luxury goods, especially if the ancient madder colours are used, the small commercial output is greatly admired and justly commands high prices.

The high cost of hand-block printing encouraged the development of screen printing, in which the design is transferred to a fine silk gauze, which is lacquered in order to make it impervious where required. Originally done by hand, the gauze screen can now be made photographically. For each colour a separate screen is necessary and, in the choicest work, as many as twelve screens may be used. The cloth is stretched out on a long table provided with pegs for locating and registering the screens. The dye paste is poured on to the screen and forced through the pervious areas by the use of a squeegee roller.

Finally we come to fully automatic roller printing in which the design is engraved on to metal rollers, each colour needing a separate roll. The machine used resembles, in principle, the rotary printing presses on which newspapers are produced. The high cost of the engraved rolls makes this process suitable only for very long runs. Whichever printing process is used, the colour is fixed by steaming so as to get deep penetration, otherwise only a surface staining would be obtained.

The coming of new synthetic dyes has been of enormous value to the fabric printer, enlarging his range and enabling him to give a degree of fastness to light and washing not formerly possible.

Today the fabric printing industry is a large one and the position of chief designer is one of distinction and high salary. This, together with the fact that it is an outlet for artistic talent, makes it an attractive career for young people. Unfortunately, many of them put all the emphasis on art, ignoring the vital fact that a good design must not only please the eye; but must also be technically adapted to the cloth which is to be printed and to the dyestuffs and the technique which are to be used.

In classical China, it is said that, for the first seven years the pupil had to concentrate on monochrome washes, before being allowed to make his first essays in colour; a lesson which aspiring designers might ponder.

For a long time this twofold aspect of design was neglected and the inventors and exploiters of mass production were so in love with their own ingenuity that (not in textiles only) they produced a flood of rubbish, utterly devoid of artistic merit; hence the description 'machine made' became synonymous with trashy design.

A small band of enthusiasts, who saw no reason why good design and modern technology should not be allied, fought and at last won the battle, and today, schools of industrial design have been set up, and government funds, on a somewhat meagre scale, have been made available. Anyone who visits the Design Centre in London may see specimens of work in many materials, serving a wide range of practical purposes and showing that craftsmanship is not a memory of the Middle Ages but a living force in the modern world.

Waterproofing

When Trinculo offered to share his gaberdine with Caliban, the protection they got from heavy rain would have been negligible because all fibres absorb water freely and disperse it through their mass by capillary action.

The first successful attempt at waterproofing was made by Charles Macintosh (1766–1843). He discovered that rubber could be dissolved in naphtha and the resulting solution spread on to cloth. When the naphtha evaporated, a thin coating of rubber was left on the surface.

Technically, Macintosh's idea was a perfect solution of the problem; and the fact that his name soon described, not a process but the garment itself, shows how popular it became. Three serious drawbacks remained. The coated fabric was very heavy; it was impervious to air and so prevented the body from 'breathing', so that moisture from within was as troublesome as moisture from without, and finally, the curiously sickly odour of naphtha and rubber clung to the garment, a defect since overcome.

Free from odour, weight or stiffness, there next came an ingenious fraud, sold by its perpetrators, with what must be called a masterpiece of sardonic humour, under the name of 'Raincoat'. This depended on the discovery that wax could, by pressure and heat, be made to adhere temporarily to the surface of cotton fibres. It conferred a momentary water repellancy and a glossy finish to the cloth. After a short time the wax, which was brittle, disintegrated and the disillusioned owner found himself wearing a denim coat. Utterly discredited, this wax treatment has disappeared from the market, partly because people found out its weakness, but more because of the coming of silicone finishes. These are yet further examples of how the craftsman's range of tools has been enlarged by the scientist who, starting from the apparently foolish question, 'What is wetness?', has found out how to control it. Highly mathematical physics would be involved in a full discussion on this matter, but the following examples will serve to illustrate the basic principles. Newton in his *Optics* said, 'There are, therefore, Agents in Nature able to make Particles of Bodies stick together by very strong Attractions. And it is the Business of experimental Philosophy to find them out.' The strong attractions between molecules of water explains why a small quantity of it forms, in air, a spherical drop. The outer layers are more strongly attracted to one another than they are to the molecules of the surrounding air. Also a sphere is the shape which contains the greatest mass within the smallest surface area. If the drop comes into contact with a substance to which the molecules are more strongly attracted than they are to one another, the drop will flatten out into a film and the substance is then said to be wet. A simple experiment will illustrate this; if we take a piece of glass and make it absolutely clean, then water drops will spread out into a film; but if we coat the glass with even a minute layer of oil, the drops will retain their spherical form, in other words, the water/water bond is much stronger than the water/oil bond. Silicones are substances which can be deposited from a solution on to textile fibres, altering their fundamental quality so far as water attraction is concerned. Cotton so treated behaves as though it has been greased but without any unpleasant effect on its appearance or feel and, as the silicones are firmly attached to the molecules of the cotton, the effect is permanent.

The result of these discoveries is that fabrics can now be treated so that neither their softness or air permeability are adversely affected but their affinity for water is destroyed. As so often happens, when we find substances which produce a particular effect, we soon find others which act in the opposite way; chemists have now produced a range of chemicals known as 'wetting out' agents, which enhance the attraction between fibres and liquids. These are of great value to the dyer as they assist the pentrating power of the dye liquor. Some of them have come into the kitchen as aids to washing up and a simple experiment will show how powerful their action is. If we take two glasses of water and to one of them add a few spots of washing-up liquid and then scatter small bits of cotton thread on the surface of the liquids, we shall see a marked difference in the time taken for the threads to sink; those in the pure water may float for a considerable time, whereas those in the treated water will become waterlogged and sink at once.

The 'Experimental Philosopher'

Those people who find happiness in climbing and fell walking will be familiar with that splendid garment, the anorak, which combines high water resistance with warmth and yet allows the body to breathe and so avoid the discomforts of perspiration.

Behind this garment lies a story which is an excellent illustration of partnership between pure science and craftsmanship.

It starts with a scientist called Peirce who, following up the line of thought suggested by Newton, asked the questions: 'If, indeed, there are Strong Attractions between particles, what is the nature of these forces when water makes cotton wet? Is it just a surface effect, as happens when glass is wetted or is the water trapped among the fibres, as it is among the pores of a sponge, or is there some more fundamental relationship?'; and finally, 'What happens when wet cotton swells?'. To each of these questions he produced answers, which were, to his brother scientists, logical and satisfactory; but, to the outside world, of no interest whatsoever, and so Peirce's essays disappeared among the archives of the Shirley Institute.

The next stage in the story did not unfold until the war came; bringing, among other problems, the national danger of devastating fires due to the incendiary bomb. This caused an overwhelming demand for fire hose which, traditionally, had been made from linen. Unfortunately, the chief sources of flax were Belgium and Russia, both of which were cut off by the enemy, so that substitutes had to be found. Cotton, or cotton coated with rubber were, for technical reasons, unsuitable; but somebody had the wit to re-read Peirce's papers and to see that, if his ideas were correct, then cotton, if spun and woven in such a way as to make use of its wetting and swelling properties, might be the answer to the problem. As so often happens, given the right compass bearings, the right path becomes obvious and before long the fire hose crisis was over.

After the war was over, the Shirley scientists had time to study what had been done and realised that the same principles, which had produced a fire hose with built-in waterproof qualities, might be applied to garment cloth; and so the Shirley Ventile fabrics were born. Light in weight and permeable to air, these automatically closed their pores when wetted and so became waterproof. Before long, a complete range of garments became available, to the great pleasure of those whose business or sport led them out of doors. The last chapter of the story came when British troops were sent to fight in Korea, an area which, the War Office failed to realise, has a winter climate of Siberian intensity. Equipped with great coats, which were similar to those esteemed by the Duke of Wellington, the troops suffered intense hardship. Returning from active service, an army officer spoke of this to a friend, who happened to be a fell walker and who gladly lent his climbing jacket for examination; with the result that, after long deliberation, the modern combat jacket was evolved.

The Prime Minister (Nottingham, September 1966) rebuked scientists and technologists for their alleged tendency to dwell in ivory towers; but if there is a moral to be drawn from the story of Peirce, and the spinners and weavers who brought his work to fruition, it is that, perhaps, the fault lies with those who cannot, or would not, see research institutes as buildings of brick and mortar and fitted with door knockers, for the use of those who wish to take more positive action towards research than a vague and perfunctory genuflexion in the church of Experimental Philosophy.

CHAPTER SIX
Carpets

IN Chapter 1 a brief reference was made to pile weaving as one of the fabric techniques used by the weaver, and although a few oriental types are made with flat weft and so come in the category of tapestry weaving, most carpets are examples of pile fabric; that is to say, the decorative effect is produced by threads which stand at right angles to the surface of the foundation cloth. Light is reflected therefore in a complicated manner and the depth of the pile gives a degree of colour saturation unequalled in any other textile; this, together with the fact that light and shade effects change according to the angle from which the material is viewed, gives carpets a sumptuous effect which is their chief beauty.

The fact that nowadays the word carpet signifies a floor covering and therefore involves durability and resistance to abrasion, may cause us to forget that in the East the original carpets were designed to be used as wall hangings, prayer mats and saddle cloths. Even as late as the 17th century Dutch interior pictures show what are clearly recognisable as Persian rugs being used both as wall hangings and table cloths.

In spite of the apparently great diversity of qualities, carpets fall into two main groups; those such as Wilton, Axminster and Brussels, which are all made by the loom in which two warps are used, the one of fine plain yarn which weaves with a similar weft to form the canvas back, while the other of coarser and softer yarn is raised to form loops which, if cut to make tufts, give Axminster and Wilton and, if left uncut, give Brussels carpet. The other group—popularly known as Persian—are made by hand, each separate tuft of pile being knotted round a pair of warp threads, each row of tufts being locked in place by a single or double pick of plain weft; but so dense is the pile formed by the knotted tufts that this ground fabric is completely concealed. A small number of oriental carpets are smooth faced that is to say the weft, which is of thick thread, is either put in by a tapestry weave or made to float over several warp ends and then wrapped completely round a single warp thread.

Hand-Knotted Carpets

Because historically they are the oldest and technically the simplest, yet the most versatile in decorative possibilities, these can be studied first. The loom consists of two strong uprights carrying a pair of rolls, the upper one supplying the warp and the lower one gathering up the completed work. Shedding is controlled by a simple bar carrying a series of loops, each of which passes round alternate warp threads, so that by drawing the bar forward the warp is separated into two layers. A simple shuttle carrying fine weft is passed by hand from side to side of the work whenever a binding pick is required. Everything then is dependent on the dexterity of the weaver's fingers. Pile, which usually is of wool, but which may be of silk or cotton, is cut into short pieces each about 2 inches long and these are knotted round two warp threads. Figure 18 shows the two types of knot, the Ghiordes or Turkish and the Sehna or Persian. As each knot is inserted separately there is no limit to the number of colours which can be used. The quality and design are governed entirely by the skill and patience of the weaver, and a measure of this can be formed from the fact that some of the finest oriental rugs may contain as many as 400 tufts per square inch. European hand tufting varies from 9 to 30 per square inch.

When a row of tufts and a pick of weft have been inserted, the fabric is beaten up with a heavy comb; this, because the force of the blows will vary, causes a slight irregularity in the work, which is considered to be one of the desirable features of hand-knotted carpets.

Sir Winston Churchill, when accused by a political opponent of having changed his ideas on some topic or other, is said to have replied, 'To change is to improve and to change often is to be perfect'. This witticism is typical of modern western philosophy;

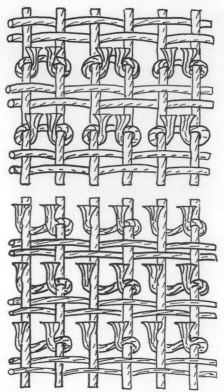

Figure 18. Ghiordes (above) and Sehna Knots used in oriental carpets

but to the people of the orient it would smack of heresy. To them the preservation of tradition and a reverence for classical ideas rank among the highest virtues. Nowhere is this more obvious than in the hand-made carpets and rugs which were made in Turkey, Persia, India and Chinese Turkestan, where each locality having adopted a particular design, colour range or technique of weaving, preserved it unchanged over long periods of time. It is by a study of these points that experts can identify with considerable accuracy the source of any particular specimen.

Some weavers used one or other of the two knots, Ghiordes or Sehna, which they bound into place by one, two or three picks of weft of a standard colour. Wool, silk and cotton being indigenous materials were characteristic of different districts.

Anything produced more than a century ago must certainly have been dyed with natural dyestuffs. Even after the discovery of aniline dyes the traditional materials continued to be used for a long time. Climate and soil therefore had a strong influence on the range of colours used in different areas.

The rich colouring of Persian and Turkish work conceals from us the extremely limited range of materials on which the old dyers exercised their skill. Kermes, known in the time of Moses as tole or tolaschani, was the dried egg of a wingless insect that fed on the leaves of the kermes oak; it gave a range of brilliant reds while brownish reds and browns were obtained from the Madder root. Indigo, which grows freely in India, Asia and Egypt was the source of all blues, while a range of clear yellows could be obtained from Persian berries, the fruit of a species of blackthorn which grows in Turkey and in the Levant. Sumach and turmeric were also used for yellow and orange shades. Kutch or Catecha, made from the wood of a species of acacia tree which flourishes in India, gave a range of beautiful browns, especially on cotton. Mordants such as iron, tin salts and alum not only fixed the colours but enabled the dyer to derive a range of tints from each basic raw material. Double dipping, i.e. the use of two successive dye baths was also practiced and was the basis of secondary colours such as purple, wine red, orange and green. Improbable as it might seem from their natural appearance, lichens are a source of a wonderful range of dyes; Cudbear gives red purple and rose pink shades, while Orchil which comes from Asia Minor is the base from which purples can be produced. This limited list of materials is the palette from which the old dyers, by the exercise of wonderful skill in manipulation, produced the traditional colours used in carpet weaving.

It was, however, in the matter of design that tradition was most strongly felt. Naturally, because the shape of the rug was usually rectangular, a border was used to frame the pattern and here the designs were of two types, geometrical forms of the 'Greek key type' and sinuous curves based on the trailing vine, while the centre panel could be divided into panels which were square, oblong or hexagonal or decorated with elaborate medallions set on a groundwork of closely intertwined foliage, stems and flowers.

The famous Ardabil Carpet, the original of which is in the Victoria and Albert Museum, but which has been reproduced in modern Wilton form, shows how all these basic design forms were combined in a delightful mixture of geometrical forms and natural floral effects.   So tenaciously were these designs preserved by different districts that an expert has little difficulty in identifying the place of origin of any particular specimen.

As we move eastwards through Chinese Turkestan to China itself the designs and textures undergo a marked change, the pile is fine, lustrous and dense, and silk is often used; colours become paler and more delicate, flower forms such as the peony are treated in a realistic manner and are so arranged as to leave large areas of plain ground.   The special feature distinguishing the Chinese work is the habit of shaving the pile with razors along the outlines of the design so as to form a fairly deep groove, which gives an appearance of carving in low relief.

Between the 14th and 17th centuries there was a carpet industry in Spain.   It is interesting to see how designs were affected by there being thus, owing to the long Moorish domination, a frontier between two cultures.   Many carpets were clearly copied from Turkish designs although the knotting was modified, a single warp end was used and as many as three picks were inserted after each row of knots; but the other designs were clearly western in form and often included elaborate heraldic devices.

Owing to the immense amount of labour which goes into a hand-made carpet there is little production left in Europe today, but in Donegal there is a small but vigorous industry, most of its productions being specially designed in consultation with architects for the decoration of company board rooms, government offices and embassies.   The fact that these carpets are designed to please individual patrons means that coats of arms and other heraldic devices are often incorporated.   An interesting and somewhat revolutionary development has however come out of this Irish school as a result of the work of a young contemporary Hungarian designer who realised that the traditional picture-frame form of border was not necessary; nor was there any need for designs to be formal in treatment. The result has been a series of patterns which are a delightful change.

Designs are impressionistic treatment of highly coloured subjects such as birds, done in vivid colours and flowing right up to the edge of the rug. This breakaway from the geometrical patterns which have dominated carpet design for so long is so pleasing that one would like to see more young designers following this line of development.

Hand-made carpets being inherently costly, together with the fact that most of the finest work was done two or three hundred years ago, has made them valuable antiques and so has naturally made them a subject for the forgers' misplaced ingenuity.

Glycerine, bleaching powder and hot irons can in a few hours simulate the effect of the knees of generations of devout Moslems praying towards Mecca, or of nomadic chieftains pitching their tents in the deserts of Arabia. Anyone therefore who is offered a bargain in Persian rugs should be deeply suspicious; as in all antiques one should deal only with people of high repute.

Many attempts have been made to reproduce by machinery the true hand-knotted pile, with little success, but the weaver's skill on the loom has evolved the modern carpet which is made by a totally different technique.

By combining the flexibility of the Jacquard machine as a pattern-making device with very ingenious forms of fabric construction, the modern carpet weaver is able to produce work which equals in fineness, beauty and durability the best hand weaving, but is within the reach of most people's pocket. If the title of master craftsman is a valid one, then the carpet weaver can justifiably lay claim to it.

The problem of combining an ordinary warp and weft fabric with other threads standing at right angles to the surface, has been solved in three main ways. Wilton, Axminster and Chenille, each of which is a separate technique giving us the names of the main groups of carpets.

In Wilton carpets two warps are used, the first is of cotton, jute or linen, which interweaves with a weft of similar yarn to form a foundation canvas and also to trap the threads of the second warp which is of worsted and contributes the colour effects to the pile. The strength and rigidity of the fabric being provided by the first warp means that the pile warp can weave in a free manner, dictated only by the requirements of the pattern. Those threads that are not being used at any particular point lie concealed and unwoven in the body of the carpet where they form stuffers.

Figure 19 shows a section view of a small unit of design woven on the Wilton principle. At each point of the design there are from one to five pile threads, any one of which can be lifted to the surface by a Jacquard harness together with an odd or even thread of ground warp.

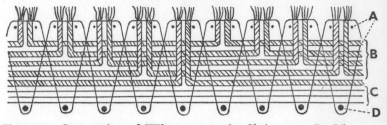

Figure 19. Cross-section of Wilton carpet. A=Chain warp, B=Pile warp, C=Stuffers, D=Weft

Two operations then take place, a shuttle is passed across to bind the fabric and a wire is inserted under all the raised pile threads so that, when they are allowed to fall, loops are formed which are afterwards cut to form tufts by a small razor-sharp knife attached to the end of the wire. The ground or chain warp is supplied by a beam as in conventional weaving, but the pile threads come from frames or creels carrying bobbins arranged in any desired sequence; the number of frames can be as high as five and this means that along any longitudinal line any one of the five colours can be employed at will. As any one frame can carry an assortment of colours, these can be varied across the fabric. It is by a combination of these two variants that the rich colouring of a Wilton carpet can be obtained.

The fact that, when not on the surface, the threads are still inside the body of the fabric means that Wilton carpet is costly,

20. THE MULE. The cycle of operation is first, the drawing out of yarn from the supply bobbins by the forward movement of the carriage against which the spinner is leaning, secondly, the insertion of twist by rotation of the spindles, and thirdly, the winding-up during the return journey of the carriage. The faller mechanism is operated by the curved arms under the spinner's hand. These shift the yarn from twisting to winding position.

The Textile Council

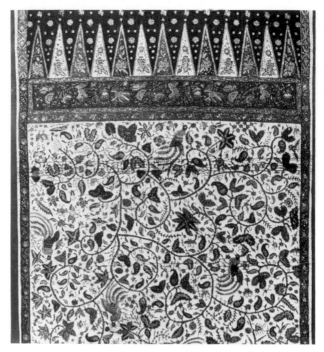

21. BATIK WORK. Except in those places where a colour was required the fabric was protected by wax when dyed. For each colour a fresh waxing was needed.

Victoria & Albert Museum, Crown Copyright. 628–1891

22. PLATE PRINTED COTTON. An enlarged detail from a picture *Vues et Sites de La Vallée.* French, 1818.

Victoria & Albert Museum, Crown Copyright. T 23–1963

23. GOLCONDA WORK, Indian, 17th century. The design
was first stencilled in monochrome and afterwards painted by hand
with mordant which, when the dye was applied, caused exceptional
fastness of colour.

Victoria & Albert Museum, Crown Copyright. 687–1898.

24. DRAW LOOM BROCADE. Weaving enriched with embroidery. French,
18th century. Note the light and shade variations produced by employing a
variety of weaves. *Victoria & Albert Museum, Crown Copyright.* 112–1880

25. PERSIAN EMBROIDERED CARPET, 19th century. The garden
filled with flowers and birds was a favourite subject for Persian designers.
Victoria & Albert Museum, Crown Copyright. 463–1895

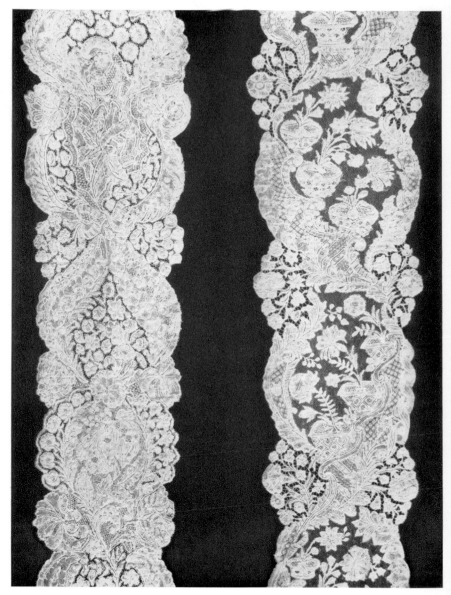

26. BOBBIN LACE LAPPETS, 18th century.   These returned to fashion in the Victorian period and hung down from either side of a lace cap.   They are shown in Whistler's portrait of his mother.

Victoria & Albert Museum, Crown Copyright.   T 14–1935 & T 66–1936

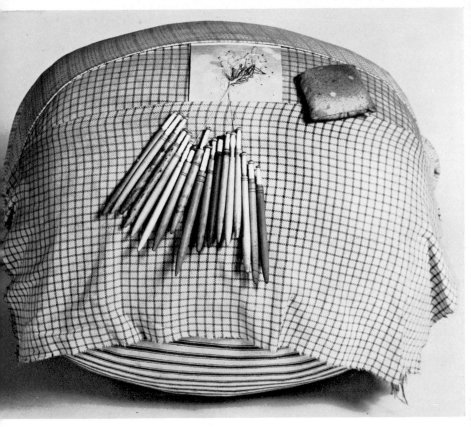

27. THE LACE-MAKER'S PILLOW, Honiton, early 19th century.
Victoria & Albert Museum, Crown Copyright. 1026–1905

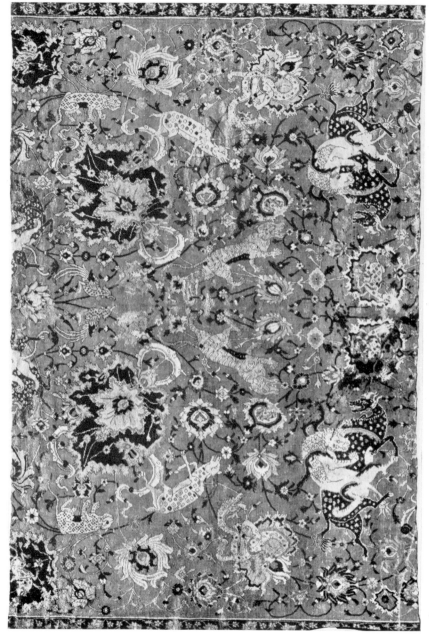

28. PERSIAN CARPET. Note the ingenious use of flower and animal forms. Turkish designs were always geometrical owing to the Moslem religious ban on 'images'. *Victoria & Albert Museum, Crown Copyright.* 670–1896

29. OPUS ANGLICANUM. Small section from the Butler Bowden Cope. This medieval embroidery was esteemed all over Europe.

Victoria & Albert Museum, Crown Copyright. T 36–1935

30. MODERN EMBROIDERY. Designed and worked by Mrs. Norman Allen
Leamington Spa. Worked entirely in white on fine black barathea this is an interestir
example of complex stitchwork, and owes much of its charm to the wide range of threa
sizes.   *Mrs. Norman All*

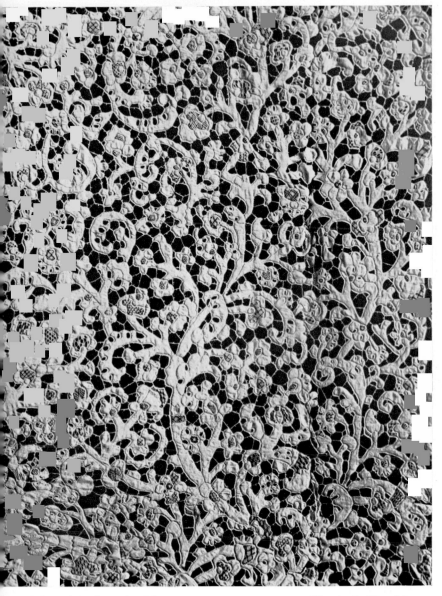

31. IRISH LACE from Carrickmacross. *Victoria & Albert Museum*

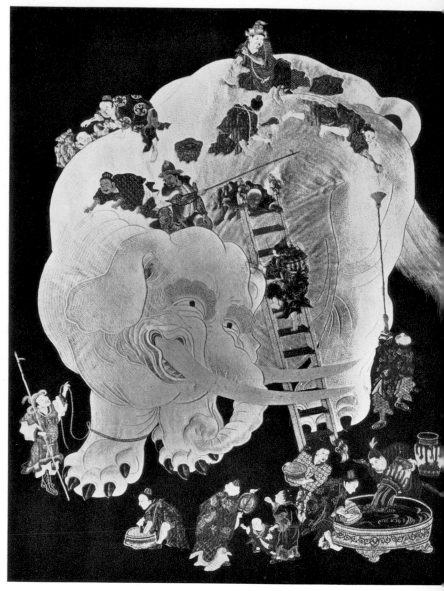

32. JAPANESE EMBROIDERY, 18th century

'Gamboll'd before them th' unwieldy elephant
To make them mirth us'd all his might
And wreath'd his lithe proboscis.'   (Milton)

Victoria & Albert Museum, Crown Copyright.   T 94–19?

3. HAND-KNOTTING A CARPET. This method, used all over the world for centuries, is here seen being carried out today by young weavers at Killibegs in Co. Donegal, Ireland.

Donegal Carpets Ltd.

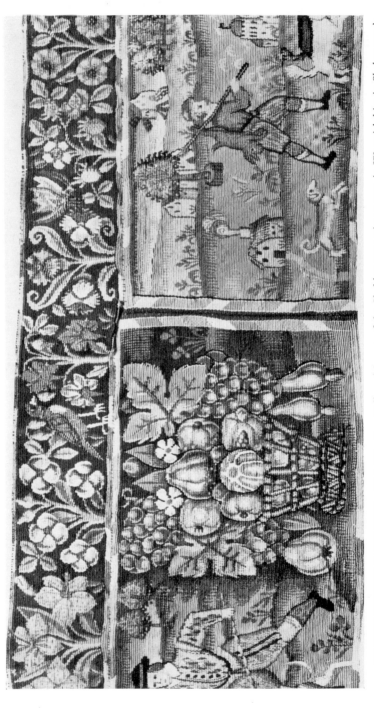

34. WARWICKSHIRE TAPESTRY. This 'Hunting Vallance' is one of the Sheldon tapestries woven in Warwickshire in Shakespeare's time. *Victoria & Albert Museum, Crown Copyright.* T 117–1934

35. MODERN JACQUARD WORK. Woven in rayon by Wm. Franklin & Son of Coventry, this was a specially designed ribbon cut by Princess Elizabeth, now Her Majesty the Queen, when she opened the new Coventry City Centre.

Wm. Franklin & Son Ltd.

36. GOBELIN TAPESTRY, Newby Hall, Yorkshire. Designed by Adam and woven by the Gobelin factory at its best period, this tapestry is shown still in use in the room for which it was designed.   *Bertram Unné & Major Edward Compton*

but the fineness of the texture is so great that it more than compensates for this drawback. As fine quality Wiltons may contain from 90 to 120 points or tufts per square inch very intricate designs with sharply defined outlines can be produced.

Although the drawing shows the pile at right angles to the cloth, it has in practice a slight cant to one side owing to the way in which the threads come to the surface, this can be detected by brushing the hand across the surface when it can both be felt and seen by the mark which is made. This characteristic of Wilton is also bound up with the tendency for hearth rugs to creep; pressure of the foot on the rug presses the pile downwards and sideways so that a succession of presses causes a ratchet action, thus moving the rug sideways. Those who complain of this minor trouble should comfort themselves with the thought that only carpets of the finest quality behave in this way.

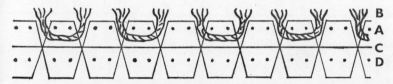

Figure 20. Cross-section of Axminster carpet. A and D: Wefts, B: Pile, C: Stuffer

The Axminster carpet is made by quite a different method which involves two distinct mechanisms, a conventional loom in which warp and weft are made into a ground fabric and a spool device which inserts at one operation a complete row of pile tufts right across the width of the loom. Each thread from a spool is passed through a tube somewhat like a hypodermic needle. The action of the device is in three stages, first the needles push the pile threads down among the warp, a shuttle passes and locks them in position and finally the needles slightly withdraw, leaving behind the second leg of a tuft. A broad knife then severs all the threads, leaving a row of tufts in the carpet (Figure 20). The spool, which is part of an endless chain, then moves away and the next spool is brought into position. The whole operation is somewhat like the method of

H

making rugs by means of a hook as practiced by many amateurs and, if one imagines a bar carrying as many hooks as there are tufts in a row being thrust forward so that all the hooks operate at the same time, then one has a general idea of how spool Axminster looms work.

The preparation of the spools is a long and complicated operation because each one is in effect a warp beam carrying a striped warp the colour sequence of which corresponds to one shuttle pick and one row of tufts. The number of spools is therefore very large and the conveyor chains which bring them forward to the operating point have to be looped and festooned in lofty frames mounted over the loom. As each tuft is a separate unit, i.e. the threads do not run along when not in use, as is the case with Wilton carpet, a special stuffer warp is used to increase the weight and density of the fabric.

At the beginning of this section we noted that at one time fine rugs were used as table cloths, and those whose childhood was spent in an Edwardian home, may recall that when the white demask cloth had been taken off the dining table it was replaced by a soft pile cloth, usually plain in colour which, in accordance with the taste of the period, was deep crimson or green but occasionally had a marbled effect with mixed colours.

Known as Chenille this fabric, according to the type of yarn used may therefore be either a carpet or a cloth and its name—French for caterpillar—gives a clue to its construction; the weft looks like a hairy caterpillar. If we pick a smoker's pipe-cleaner to pieces we shall find that it consists of a pair of fine wires twisted together, and that these entrap short lengths of fluffy thread which stick out like bristles at right angles to the axis of the wire. If we replace the wires by two or three strands of fine warp yarn we have a chenille thread.

In practice chenille is made in a loom which has its fine cotton warp threads split into groups spaced half an inch or so apart. Coloured wool weft is then put across; when the fabric is woven it passes over knives which separate it into strips, each group of warp ends having tufts of weft sticking out on either side. The strips are then steamed and set by passing them over a grooved roller, thus causing the tufts to assume a V form, and are wound on to spools.

A second loom then takes over and has a normal warp and weft weaving a ground fabric and a second warp which is fine and sparse, and a second shuttle carrying the chenille thread which is tacked down on to the surface of the cloth. If the original thread fabric is woven with multi-coloured weft stripes the chenille will, when cut, exhibit bands of colour and, provided the sections are matched up in the second loom, patterns and shapes can be formed.

This may to the layman be slightly reminiscent of G. K. Chesterton's 'The night we went to Birmingham by way of Beachy Head', but the final effect is rather charming and at least deserves a brief mention as one of the curiosities of weaving. Embroiderers were quick to see the possibilities of chenille as an unusual material which, although it could not be threaded through a needle and stitched in the normal way, could nevertheless be laid on the surface of a smooth fabric and tacked down by couching. The final effect was to give a raised plush ornament, or, if very fine net was used as the foundation, pierced velvet effect.

CHAPTER SEVEN

Embroidery, Lace and Needlework

UNLIKE weaving in which, as we have seen, mechanical ingenuity was the key to progress, we now come to a group of products where finger dexterity is the very essence of the matter. If price is any measure of quality then the craft of lace-making must take pride of place; in 1763 the lace hangings for the bed at the christening of the Duke of York cost £3,783, and in 1867 M. Lefebure exhibited two flounces valued at £3,400 which represented the work of forty women for seven years.

Embroidery was equally precious and some of the finest English work, known as Opus Anglicanum, was bought by Popes for the vestments at St. Peter's in Rome, and so great was the labour involved that often the people who started a work did not live to see it finished. Yet the lace makers' or embroiderers' tools were of the greatest simplicity. Needles, scissors, pins and small bone bobbins were all the worker needed. While it is true today that much of the lace and embroidery sold in shops is made by machinery, nevertheless the choicest work is still done by hand. It is the devoted skill of amateurs which keeps alive these examples of textile craftsmanship.

Chapter 26 of the Book of Exodus gives such precise details of the hangings of the Tabernacle that a modern embroiderer would have no difficulty in reproducing them.

One of the best-known specimens of textile art is the Bayeux tapestry; this is not a woven but an embroidered fabric.

Chaucer says:

> And in overgilt samite
> y-clad she was by great delite.

which means that a satin fabric, undoubtedly of real silk, was embroidered with gold thread.

Garments portrayed in ancient Egyptian pictures are clearly made of lace net.

A technical description of the multitude of different types of needlework is quite beyond the scope of a single chapter, but a few general notes and a short description of a small selection of some of the most famous work will at least serve to show the degree of artistic skill and craftsmanship involved.

Embroidery

All types of embroidery have one feature in common, they are decorative effects produced by stitches on a foundation fabric, previously woven on the loom and because the embroiderer is not restricted by the requirements of fabric geometry and structure, there is a freedom of choice of material and in the placing of stitches which is denied to the weaver. Warp and weft must of necessity intersect at right angles, but the embroiderer is free to lay stitches at any angle according to the nature of the design and, because a change of colour only involves picking up another needle, there is no limit to the number of colours which can be employed. Nor does the thickness of the thread present any difficulty because heavy corded threads or even metal wire can be laid on the surface of the cloth, being held in place by fine binding stitches. That the same part of the design can be worked over several times, first with thick padding thread and then with fine decorative silk, means that high relief work is possible and it is this three dimensional effect which gives some embroidery its sumptuous effect. Ecclesiastical vestments and altar frontals are beautiful examples of this type of work. The illuminations of the Book of Kells, apart from their own beauty as works of art, give a wonderful picture of the richness of texture and vigour of design which marked the work of the 9th century.

The Bayeux tapestry is a work of quite a different kind being outline work done in chain stitch on a linen ground and using only eight colours of wool for the design. The realism of the line drawings portraying the story is relieved by a delightful freedom in the choice of colour, so blue or yellow horses with parti-coloured legs contribute to the total effect.

The freehand style arising from the simple chain stitch is in marked contrast with the more rigid forms which appear when canvas is used as the foundation and the pattern is formed by stitches which are carefully counted out, producing work such as gros point, petit point and the Berlin wool work much beloved by the Victorian ladies. Naturalism here depends entirely on the fineness and closeness of the stitches and on subtle gradations of colour. The overall effect closely resembles that of woven tapestry but even to the naked eye the difference between the weaver's and embroiderer's stitches is clearly perceptible. Raised effects are not possible because the same type of stitch and the same thickness of yarn must be used in all parts of the design.

Like the music of the harpsichord, which an unkind critic likened to someone playing on a bird cage with a toasting fork, stitch embroidery has a certain monotony and one greets with joy the opening words of Mary Hogarth's book, *Modern Embroidery*, where she says, 'The technique should be governed by the design', and so one finds Marian Stoll in her *The Storm* using an informal split stitch to give the same dynamic quality as an artist's heavy impasto; whereas Emmie Anderson, by combining American oil cloth, Woolworth's pink rubber sheeting and floss silk, creates a picture of cherubs, stars and flowers which has all the freshness and gaiety of an early Italian painting. The piece was intended as a decoration for a child's bathroom and makes one feel that the designer brought about that happy union between idea and execution which is so difficult to achieve.

The same delicate skill that enables the Chinese to excel in ivory carving and the painting of porcelain, finds expression in embroidery, and a visit to any museum having a collection of Chinese art including textiles is most profitable. Screens, wall hangings and ceremonial robes are all decorated with magnificent embroidery of exquisite fineness and complexity.

The delicacy of the stitchwork which characterises Chinese embroidery is enhanced by the wonderful range of colours the dyers were able to produce, partly because silk is of all fibres the most readily dyed with the whole colour spectrum, but even more because the Chinese dyers had brought their art to a standard of perfection higher than anything achieved elsewhere. Many of the subtle pastel shades used in China are the result of complex colour blending.

The other characteristic feature of this embroidery is due to another property of silk, its high tensile strength even before it is twisted. This makes it possible to use floss silk, the filaments of which lie parallel to one another; thus is formed a soft bulky thread which, when used in embroidery, produces a grainless surface resembling enamel in solidity of colour and lustre.

In complete contrast to the highly stylised Chinese work is the example of modern work done by Mrs. Allen of Leamington (Plate 30) who, using a very wide range of stitches and knots, but restricting herself to white on black barathea, has designed and executed a light and airy piece of work.

Apart from the rich variety of stitches used, this design also shows a wide range of threads, from fine string down to 300's cotton, so fine that a pound would contain a quarter of a million yards. These technical points are however less important than the design itself, which is an excellent example of original and creative work based on craftsmanship—pencil and paper, if they were used, can only have served to make a note of what had originated by an alliance of finger dexterity and artistic feeling.

Embroidery seems to have originated in Asia Minor and was known as Phrygium after the Phrygians who were specially adept in this art. Homer has many descriptions of garments and hangings which were the work of Helen of Troy, Andromache and Penelope. For a long time the Romans imported embroidery from the Middle East and Cicero speaks of the magnificence of the robes worn by Tarquin the Elder, which, he says, were of Babylonian workmanship. As the Romans became richer and more cultured they began to practice the art themselves. We find that silk-woven fabrics were imported from China and unpicked for the sake of the thread which the Roman ladies used

in their work.   So jealously was the secret of this choice material
guarded by the Chinese that this was the only means of obtaining
it.

We can infer that a great school of embroidery must have
grown up in Rome, because the various types of stitchwork were
recognised and named.   Thus we get Opus Consutum which
means the stitching of pieces of fabric cut out to shapes and applied
decoratively to the base cloth; this is now known as appliqué
work.   Opus Plumarium was done in satin stitch and resembled
the plumage of birds, while Opus Pulvinarium was stitchwork
on canvas.

From Rome the art spread to England where the women
showed outstanding skill and developed a characteristic style of
their own, known as Opus Anglicanum.   So highly was this
valued and admired that churches and monasteries all over Europe
counted specimens of Opus Anglicanum among their treasures.

For some mysterious reason historians tended to suggest that
after the fall of Rome there followed five or six centuries, which
they dismissed as the Dark Ages, during which civilisation
languished in a world dominated by barbarians, but there is
abundant evidence that, whatever may have happened in the
political sphere, craftsmanship and artistic skill continued to
flourish.   Anglo-Saxon embroidery, illuminated texts such as
the Book of Kells and the work of the Irish goldsmiths all tell the
same story; it was an age of great aesthetic vigour and growth.
Both the quality of the workmanship and the originality of the
designs speak to us over a gap of more than a thousand years,
telling a story of men and women who were inspired by a deep
love of beauty which was intimately bound up with their religious
faith.   Whatever scientific humanism may have done for man-
kind, it is extremely doubtful whether it will leave behind a
legacy of splendid work such as we have inherited from the
so-called Dark Ages.

During the 18th and 19th centuries there arose a second *opus
anglicanum* which seems to have been a product of infinitely
laborious stitchwork and evangelical piety.   Completely devoid
of artistic merit, the sampler was produced by the slave labour of

little girls who were forced by their elders to enshrine in cross stitch such extraordinary thoughts as the following.

> Our days, alas, our mortal days
> Are short and wretched too
> Evil and few the patriarch said
> And well the patriarch knew.
>   Esther Tabor, 1771
>
> Oh may thy powerful word
> Inspire a breathing worm
> To rush into thy Kingdom Lord
> And take it as by storm.
>   Sarah Beckett, 1798, aged 8

It was somewhere between Esther and Sarah producing these strange thoughts that young Mr. Wordsworth said:

> Bliss was it in that dawn to be alive
> But to be young was very heaven!

but he was thinking of the storming of the Bastille and not the invasion of heaven by high-speed worms.

Lace

If we study the diagrams of various woven fabrics in Chapter 1 we shall see that the nature of the interweaving of warp and weft is such that they must be closely packed together if the fabric is to have firmness and stability, the two qualities which are essential if it is to be useful. This means that openwork effects are either impossible in weaving or can only be achieved by difficult techniques which severely limit the decorative possibilities. If, however, widely spaced threads, when they do intersect, can be locked together by some form of knot then open structure and rigidity can be combined. Darning with a needle or plaiting by means of bobbins are the two methods by which this can be achieved. Valenciennes, Brussels and Alençon are great examples of needle stitchwork whilst Honiton and Mechlin are famous types of Bobbin, or, because the work is carried out on a framework of pins stuck into a pad, Pillow lace.

The first operation in all needlepoint laces is the tracing of the design on to a piece of parchment, on which the design is first drawn and then pricked out with a needle that makes a pair of closely spaced holes at each step of the outline. Two needles are then used, the one carrying a coarse and the other a fine thread, and these are worked alternately to form short chains and long chain stitches connecting the holes. The effect of this is to make a running chain which forms the outline and foundation of the work. Two lines of development can then follow, either the spaces of the outline can be filled with fine honeycomb network which looks, because of the fineness of the thread, like gauze, or made solid by various types of buttonhole stitch. Plate 31 shows a splendid example of this type of lace.

The working of the ground net calls for the most exquisite skill, because not only must the meshes be absolutely uniform in size but the tension on the thread must never vary, otherwise cockling and distortion will disfigure the work. After the small units of design have been made separately they are joined together by almost invisible stitches to form a large piece of lace such as a collar. Each of these operations called for a specialised skill and so a finished work was a piece of team work. So we find that at Alençon in the reign of Louis XIV the workers were distinguished by such names as the *traceuse* who set out the design, the *reseleuse* who worked the ground net. Flat filling in was done by the *remplisseuse* but raised work was left to the *brodeuse*. The joining of the pieces was supervised by the *assembleuse* but she had specialist assistants known as *toucheuse, brideuse* and *boucleuse*, each of whom carried out one operation.

Fortunately the great portrait painters of the 17th century lavished as much care on the garments of their subjects as they did on the actual features and so we have a record of the masterpieces of the lace maker's art, a full appreciation of which can only be made by studying the stitches with a magnifying glass; but their full beauty can only be seen when they are shown in use as sumptuous ornament.

In all true point laces no other implement than the needle was used, but pillow or bobbin laces of equal fineness and complexity called for slightly more elaborate methods but equally great delicacy of touch and infinity of patient labour.

Just as in needlepoint work, so in pillow lace the design was traced on parchment and the key intersection points pricked in with a needle, but no 'fil de trace' or outline thread was used; instead, a number—sometimes several hundred threads—each wound on a small bone bobbin, were used and these were interwined and plaited in a variety of ways to form an open mesh or ground, the spacing of which was controlled by pins stuck into the holes made in the parchment. Like the dancers of a corps de ballet the bobbins twist and turn in rhythmic pattern and although the total effect is one of great complexity the basic steps are few and simple. Figure 21 shows four of these.

In A we have the simplest ground form in which adjacent pairs of bobbins are twisted to form a cable thread, but this does not, in itself, make a fabric. In B, however, we have introduced a traversing motion by transposing the second and third threads so that a diamond mesh is created. By repeating this change of order a thread may be made to progress a step at a time from first to last position.

In order to make a fancy pattern, however, this progression must be either stopped or reversed and in order to do this an anchor point is necessary and this is provided by the insertion of a pin as shown at C. Below the pin a new sequence of change can be introduced and, once it is established the pin can be withdrawn.

As in most laces the pattern is made up of solid effects on an open network ground, some method of darning is necessary and D shows this.

In the making of a complex pattern a very large number of bobbins will be involved and, because the worker has only one pair of hands, some means must be devised whereby those threads which are not at any particular moment being manipulated can be kept in order, and this is the function of the pillow, into which pins can easily be stuck and on which the bobbins can hang until they are to be manipulated.

Plate 27 shows a lace-maker's pillow garnished with its pins and bobbins the latter being coloured for identification purposes; some are ground network threads while others either interweave

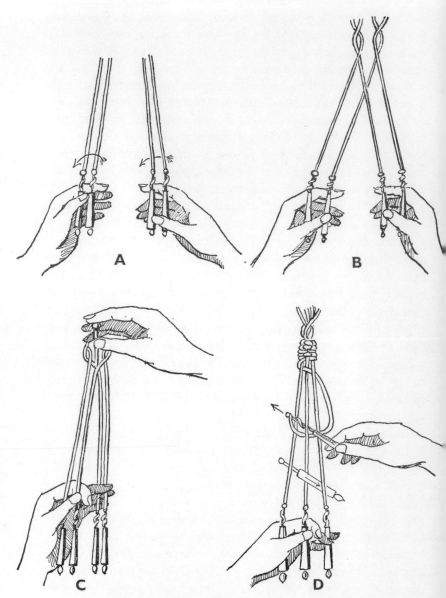

Figure 21. Basic movements in pillow lace making

as a ground weft or locking thread, while others work in a more free style to produce ornamental effects.

Each of the great classical schools of lace making had its characteristic system of stitches and designs the use of which was governed by strict rules. Experts can, therefore, identify the work done by the various centres.

Plate 26 shows specimens of a few of the finest laces, each typical of one of the great lace-making traditions.

The intricacy of the lace worker's art was such that it could only be an object of high luxury; the invention of machinery put an end to hand lace-making as an economic activity.

A few devoted amateurs still keep it alive, however, as a craft skill and in recent years there has been a marked revival of interest in this beautiful work. They should, however, look upon their apparently harmless activity as one fraught with some peril when they consider the fate which overtook the lace makers of Chantilly. The frenzied mob of the French Revolution failed to distinguished between lace wearers, who were the hated aristocrats, and the lace makers who were industrious artisans and so all were sent to the guillotine together. By 1805, however, wiser councils prevailed and Napoleon realised that revolutionary theory and sumptuous garments were not incompatible and so re-established the craft in its ancient home.

Netting and Knotting

It is interesting and amusing to note that Dr. Johnson when called upon to define the complex art of weaving gave us a phrase of crystal clarity; but when he studied the oldest and simplest example of textile craftsmanship, the net, defined it as, 'Anything reticulated or decussated at equal distances, with interstices between the intersections'.

Unlike weaving or lace-making, both of which involve a multiplicity of threads, the net is formed by a single cord looped and knotted upon itself, the shape of the loops being maintained by the knot which is tied at each intersection. Two simple tools only are involved, the needle and the mesh; the former being a long slip of wood forked at both ends to that yarn can be wound on it and carried through the loops, the latter being a rod or flat strip round which they are formed, their size being regulated by its diameter or width.

Once the basic principle of looping and knotting had been invented it soon became clear that there was no need always to link each new loop to the previous one in simple progression, but that elaborate ornamental effects could be made by complex interlocking of the loops. Closely allied to net-making is the art of tatting in which the needle is replaced by a pointed shuttle. In the Victorian period tatting was very popular and elaborate designs made from fine thread were produced, many of them resembling fine lace in appearance.

Nearly all primitive peoples were familiar with netting, valuing it as a useful art because it provided the means whereby small animals or birds or, better still, fish could be trapped. The economic value of a simple means of getting food must have been enormous to those who had not yet developed the idea of keeping domesticated animals; but, as always seems to happen, decoration goes hand in hand with utility. Just as the early potters embellished their work by scratching designs on the surface or by introducing colour effects, so the net-maker developed his ingenious idea for aesthetic purposes.

Ancient Egyptian paintings show people dressed in netting tunics often formed from bright coloured silks. Amasis, King of Egypt, gave a netted corslet to Mutianus the third Roman Consul, and Herodotus admired the fineness of the linen thread nets made by the Egyptians. Solomon's Temple had curtains of 'checker work' while Isaiah speaks of the cauls of network and veils worn by Jewish women and, like all puritans who see an intimate connection between beauty and sin, he specifically mentioned those who 'weave networks' as those on whom a curse would fall. Those stern moralists who today see Carnaby Street as a haunt of iniquity and decadence are in the direct line of descent from the Old Testament prophets.

By the 13th century, however, more enlightened views prevailed and lace and network, often confused by non-technical people, were so highly esteemed that they were thought fit for

shrouds of saints and altar cloths. So highly were they valued
that they were specifically mentioned in the inventories of the
treasures of cathedrals and the Vatican, and were recognised as a
separate branch of textile art under the name of Opus Filatorium
or Opus Araneum because of their resemblance to the spider's
web. Later on, netting, decorated by darning with silk or gold
wire, was known as Lacis and a specimen of this was mentioned
in the will made by Mary Queen of Scots before the birth of her
son. With the coming of the great periods of classic lace work
in the 17th and 18th centuries the art of ornamental net-work
fell into decay although in the form of tatting it had a revival in
the Victorian period. Today, net is a common article in wide
use, but is entirely machine made, and what was once treasured
as a miracle of fine craftsmanship serves to keep mosquitoes from
those who wish to enjoy peaceful sleep in the tropics; and the
word tatting, once descriptive of a gift from a king to a Roman
Consul, now survives only in the expression 'Rags and tatters'.

John Heathcoat and his Net Machine

The tedious business of twisting threads together by hand, made
bobbin lace the costly luxury it was in the period 1600–1800, and
so there was a powerful stimulus towards the invention of
machines which could perform this task mechanically.

If one studies the diagrams opposite page 125 it will be seen
that the two basic motions in the making of bobbin lace are
twisting and traversing, and any machine must therefore allow
of these two being combined at will. In spite of claims to the
contrary it was to one man, John Heathcoat, that the credit
must be given for producing a satisfactory solution of the
problem.

Born in 1783, Heathcoat was the son of a small farmer who, on
becoming blind, moved to Long Whatton near Loughborough
and invested his capital in a textile machinery business connected
with the hosiery trade; and so his son John came to be apprenticed
to this trade. By 1809 he had completed his invention and took
out a patent which, although attacked, was upheld. Heathcoat
went into partnership with a man called Gracey and they set up a

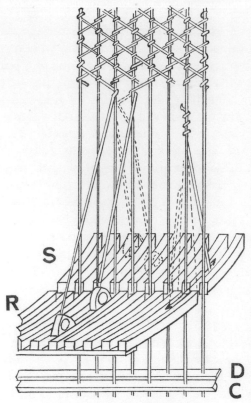

Figure 22. Heathcoat's machine

factory in Loughborough where they soon established a prosperous business; but in 1816 the factory was completely destroyed
by Luddites and the partners lost machinery worth £10,000.
Heathcoat must have been a man of exceptionally resolute
character because, undeterred by this tragedy, he went to Devon-
shire and at Tiverton established a flourishing business.

The essential parts of Heathcoat's machine can be seen in
Figure 22. It consists of two comb bars S and R placed with
their teeth facing each other but separated by a fine gap through
which pass down a series of warp threads controlled by two bars
D and C. Working in the slots of the comb bars are a series of
very thin shuttles which can be moved across the gap. The

comb bars are curved in such a way that the shuttle thread moves like the rod of a pendulum the pivot of which is situated at the point where the twisting takes place. This ensures that the working length of the thread is constant in length and therefore also in tension.

By means of cams, not shown in the diagram, both the warp bars and the combs can be 'shogged' or moved sideways, so that as the shuttles pass to and fro across the gap two things happen; either the warp thread which was to the left of a shuttle on its outward journey can be shifted to the right-hand position on the return so that a twist is inserted, or by shogging the comb bars, the shuttles can be made to traverse diagonally across the fabric, because on leaving the first slot in the comb R, it enters the first slot in S, but before it returns, the side movement causes it to come back into the second slot and so at each passage it moves one place sideways till it reaches the last slot where a switch mechanism transfers it to the other comb where it begins its crabwise journey back to its first position. We have therefore two groups of shuttles, one on each face and moving from left to right or the reverse according to which comb is moved. It is by the combination of these two motions of twisting and traversing that the diamond structure of the mesh is produced. The uniformity of the mesh is controlled by a bar which moves forward and inserts pins between the meshes, then by an upward stroke pushes them into position. The sideways traversing of the shuttles can perhaps be more clearly understood if we liken it to what happens in a railway marshalling yard, where by changing the points from left to right or the reverse, waggons can be shunted from track to track. The shogging of the comb bars acts in just the same way as this shifting of the points of the rails.

I

CHAPTER EIGHT

The Craftsman in Society

S ONIA COLE in her book *The Neolithic Revolution* points out that for half a million years men lived a nomadic life, hunting animals and gathering wild foods; but about 8000 B.C. they changed over to a settled way of life, practising agriculture, living in communities and developing the useful arts. She says, 'This sedentary and more economic way of life gave some measure of security and allowed leisure for the arts of civilisation. Enough surplus food could be accumulated to support specialised craftsmen, devoting most of their time to the manufacture of tools, pottery, clothing and buildings.'

As soon as there is an exchange of goods or services a market is created and the craftsman's relationship with the community introduces problems of prices and incomes; and, because men who practise the same art tend to form a group, bound together by common interest, society will take a lively interest in their collective activities. Only the mythical Miller of Dee could sing, 'I care for nobody, no not I; and nobody cares for me'.

As the craftsman's skill and productivity increase by experience and inventiveness, he changes and enriches the community in which he lives, thus there is established a mutually beneficial relationship between the two. Written records of what happened in ancient times are scanty; but fortunately there is a well documented history of one city in which textile craftsmen played a major part in the economy for over eight hundred years, raising it to the rank of fifth city of the kingdom and attracting the attention of a succession of Kings who, by royal charters, granted legal rights which were jealously guarded and preserved. That city is Coventry, today looked on as essentially an engineering centre, but which for over a thousand years grew to prosperity mainly by the art of the weaver and his allied craftsmen; and in so doing wrote a history of the common man establishing his place in society by manufacture, thus laying the foundations of municipal government. Long before Adam Smith wrote the *Wealth of Nations* the weavers of Coventry realised that their skill gave them a bargaining power which in turn attracted the attention of governments.

Unknown in Roman times Coventry was a small Anglo Saxon settlement in a clearing of the great forest of Arden which formed part of the Earldom of Mercia. It was Earl Leofric, husband of Lady Godiva who, with the approval of Edward the Confessor and the Pope, founded a great Benedictine Priory, among whose endowments was 'The moiety of the Villa of Coventry'.

So in 1043 the town was divided into two parts, the Prior's half and the Earl's half, thus establishing a dual government, one half of the city being under ecclesiastical and the other under civil administration.

It was to the Earl's half that in 1181 Ranulf, Earl of Chester, gave a charter whereby it became a legally established community with wide powers of self-government. The most interesting clause in the charter was that which said, 'Moreover I command that whatsoever merchants they may bring with them for the improvement of the Vill they may have peace and no one may do injury to them or unjustly send them to trial'. So before the end of the 12th century Coventry became a free trade area as well as a place of pilgrimage. By a fortunate chance two great Cistercian monasteries were established, at Combe and at Stoneleigh, each a few miles away. The Cistercians were great sheep farmers so ensuring an abundant supply of raw material for the weavers of the city. Thirty miles to the south lay the Cotswold hills, one of the greatest sheep grazing areas of England, from which even more abundant supplies of wool became available. Legal documents of the period identified a man by his occupation and so we hear of Hugh the Burler (cloth dresser), Giles le Waydour (dyer of woad), Walter le Whytewebbe (weaver of white cloth), as well as Ralph the Weaver. The importance of the weavers in the community is shown by a list of the number of armed men which each trade had to furnish to the army during the Wars of the Roses. Out of a total of 603 the three highest assessments were Tailors and Shearmen 64, Drapers 59, Weavers 57, Dyers 37, Walkers and Fullers (cloth finishers) 27. Even the Cardmakers who furnished the wire brushes for dressing the raw wool prior to spinning had to find seven soldiers. Bearing in mind how small was the population of the whole country this shows how important Coventry had become as a manufacturing centre.

It was King Edward III in agreement with his mother Queen Isabella and his son Edward the Black Prince, who finally established Coventry as a City by the granting of the Charter of 1345 under which the citizens were empowered to elect a mayor and bailiffs under whose authority the City was to be governed. It is interesting to note that the king ended the charter with the words, 'Given under our hand at Westminster the twentieth day of January in the eighteenth year of Our reign over England but the fifth over France', and also that one of the twelve signatories of the agreement on behalf of the city was Walter Whitewebb the weaver, who in 1354 became mayor.

During the 14th century Edward III and his successors, recognising the growing wealth and power of the great cities of the kingdom, granted by charter the rights of self-government to local inhabitants; and so many of the functions now exercised by the central government were left to local merchants and craftsmen. Citizenship therefore meant political and economic power and the freedom of a city was an essential qualification for a man who wished to carry on his trade.

Wherever men share a common enthusiasm or interest it is natural for them to found a society for the promotion and protection of their affairs; in the Middle Ages the formation of a guild was a natural expression of this activity. Originally the guilds were entirely religious in intent as is shown by their names. The guilds of St. Mary and St. John and The Trinity were founded by pious persons for the building of churches and chantries and for the payment of priests, among whose duties was the saying of masses for the souls of the members past and present,

and for the exercise of charitable works. So famous and powerful was the Trinity Guild that wealthy people from other parts of
the country sought membership and among its members was Sir
Richard Whittington, Lord Mayor of London. Even kings
themselves were members and Henry IV, Henry V, and Henry
VI were on the roll of members. Gradually the guilds, having
among their members many wealthy merchants, assumed economic functions, and one member John Onley after being mayor of
the city became mayor of the Staple at Calais. Women were
admitted to equal membership with men and the records show
that in 1413 Margery Russell, having lost a cargo of merchandise
worth £800 to pirates at Santander, proceeded to secure letters
of marque whereby she was authorised to equip ships and to take
retaliatory measures by seizing Spanish merchandise of equivalent
value.

Gradually the guilds developed from their original religious
and merchantile character and became attached to trade activities
and so the weavers, dyers and fullers organised themselves into
societies for the regulation of their own trade.

Membership of a trade guild was obtainable only by one
channel, apprenticeship, leading to freedom of the city; without
which no man might carry on a trade within the city boundary.
It is interesting to see how great was the emphasis placed by these
old craftsmen on quality. All cloth woven had to be taken to the
Searching House for inspection by a committee composed of two
weavers, two fullers and six drapers; who, if satisfied, attached
a seal as a guarantee of quality. Any goods failing to reach the
necessary standard were returned to the maker who was fined
6s. 8d. for his offence. Stern ordinances were issued against the
use by some dyers of inferior French dyes and against the evil
practices of some fullers who overstretched the cloth whereby the
clothiers suffered 'Great loss by these divers deceits'. Restrictive
practices were also the object of the Guild's attention and in 1424
a court of enquiry was set up to settle the question of how many
looms a master weaver might operate and how many journeymen
he might employ. It is interesting to learn that the arbitrators
gave their decision in favour of complete freedom of choice.

The rise and fall of the guilds form part of the national history of the late Middle Ages and their story is not especially relevant either to Coventry or to textiles. For a brief moment the Guild of St. George appeared and is of interest because it was founded by the journeymen who were dissatisfied with their wages and hours of work. Actively disliked both by the aristocratic Trinity Guild and by the Trade Guilds this early attempt at trade union activity had one success, it reached a settlement of the proportion of the price paid for the weaving of the cloth which was to be paid as journeymen's wages; then it faded away.

Short-lived as the Guild system was, it left behind something which in Coventry has endured and grown over a period of 600 years—the apprenticeship system.

When we read in the press that someone has received the freedom of a city, the correct assumption is that he is a distinguished statesman or commander in war; but in Coventry several hundred young men and women are given the freedom of the city for exactly the same reason as was the case in the 14th century; they have served for the requisite number of years as indentured apprentices. On the foundations laid by the medieval craftsmen, among whom the textile workers played a dominant role, a system has been cherished unaltered for 600 years and today plays an important and much esteemed role in the industrial life of the city: so well were these foundations laid that modern industries such as engineering have adopted them as the basis of their training schemes.

The story starts with a boy or girl, with the knowledge and consent of a parent or guardian, entering into a solemn legal agreement with an employer binding the three parties to observe certain duties. The employer covenants to teach the apprentice the whole mystery of the craft or trade, both in his own works and at a suitable place of education. The parent undertakes to be responsible for clothing and maintaining the boy and to be responsible for his good behaviour, while the boy promises to apply himself diligently to his studies and, as one old indenture says, 'He shall not game at games, dice at dice, or frequent taverns, but shall behave himself as a good and faithfull apprentice ought'.

Having been signed and witnessed and, in the case of a company, sealed, this indenture is then forwarded to the town clerk who enters it in a register. If by mischance the parties to the indenture fall out then it has to be officially cancelled, but so highly is the matter regarded that such a thing is extremely rare. The apprentice can not light-heartedly walk out on his obligations nor can the employer in a fit of pique or irritation get rid of him. Many large firms have a full-time apprentice supervisor, whose functions in many ways resemble those of a house master at a public school. He supervises the boy's technical studies and watches his progress through the works to see that his activities are primarily directed towards experience and training without regard to economic values.

After five, formerly seven, years the apprentice is deemed to be a trained and qualified craftsman and is ready to present himself as a candidate for the freedom of the city.

The ceremony is one of great solemnity, conducted by the Lord Mayor himself, who has the city mace placed on the table as a symbol that he is about to exercise his rights as the Queen's personal officer authorised by many ancient and royal charters. All business is conducted on oath. The apprentices accompanied by their masters, or in the case of companies a very senior official, present themselves one by one and swear that the indenture now produced is the one they signed five years ago and that they are in fact the parties to the covenant. The master then testifies that the apprentice has well and faithfully performed all the duties he undertook.

Having now satisfied himself that all the legal formalities have been observed, the Lord Mayor then calls the apprentices before him and administers the oath which every freeman must take in the following words:

The Oath of a Freeman
I do sincerely promise and swear that I will be faithful and bear true allegiance to Her Majesty the Queen. And that I will be obedient unto the Mayor and the Magistrates of this city. The lands, liberties,

franchises and lawful customs thereof I will maintain, and the same in all that I can or may lawfully defend and keep harmless. I will be tributary to all contributions, taxes, tollages, watch, summons, scot and lot, and all other charges to be laid within this city, bearing my part as any other freeman shall or ought. I will maintain and defend the Queen's peace in that I may, and if I shall know of any gatherings or conspiracies moved or made against the Queen's peace I will let the Mayor or Justices of this city know the same. I will not withhold or impair, nor conceal the withholding or impairing, of any evidences or charters belonging to this city, but will warn the Mayor or Justices of this city of the same. I will not colourably bear or seem to bear or allow any horse, mare, gelding, colt, filly, cow or heifer or cattle of any man's but of my own on any of the commons of this city. All which points and articles I do swear well and truly to keep according to the laws of God and the realm and the lawful customs of this city. So help me God

This text is worthy of study for all it implies and it shows how closely citizenship and craftsmanship were linked in the minds of those city fathers who looked on the carrying out of their rights under the Charter of 1345 as a most solemn obligation. Today, when reaching the age of 21 is the automatic admission to full citizenship and a job is looked upon as a basic human right, it is interesting to study a time when rights and obligations were inseparably linked by solemn contract.

In return for his promises under oath to be a good citizen, the freeman received valuable rights which were most jealously guarded. These rights fell under three heads: first without the freedom of the city a man might not carry on his trade; secondly, and most important in an age when craftsmanship and agriculture were twin activities, the right to enjoy the use of land for corn growing and cattle grazing; and thirdly, in old age to have a pension paid from the Seniority Fund whose income was, and is, derived from rent of land. The craftsmen had worked out a system of social security long before the words had acquired their modern meaning.

Today, although the three commons of Styvechale, Hearsall and Whitley are still open spaces within the city boundary the agricultural rights are no more than a picturesque survival, but the influence of the apprenticeship system is a powerful force in the technical educational life of the city. The majority of the full-time students at the Lanchester College of Technology are apprentices, many of whom are studying for qualifications of University Degree standard. It is interesting to note that this apprenticeship system is not restricted to sons or daughters of citizens. Anyone regardless of race, colour or creed may enter into an indenture. The liberal idea that inspired Ranulf Earl of Chester to write into his charter of 1181 the provision that strangers should enjoy peace and protection within the city, has never died. The Board of Trade statistics show an impressive list of products which flow from Coventry's factories but omit what is perhaps the most notable, the stream of highly trained and qualified men and women, enriching not only the British economy but passing overseas to all parts of the world.

Every true craftsman loves to see his precious and hard earned knowledge preserved and transmitted to a new generation, and so if Walter Whitewebb could return and sit beside the modern Lord Mayor he might justifiably claim that what has grown out of his works is a true expression of the motto of the old Weaver's Company 'Weave truth with trust'. It does not matter whether it is warp and weft or man-made fibres or jet engines or electronic devices, for the craftsman one thing matters—only the best is good enough.

The question arises, how high were the standards of workmanship and design achieved by those early weavers, and how do they compare with modern work? Because of the perishable nature of the products few actual specimens have survived, but there is a good deal of indirect evidence which goes to show that the workmanship was superb. In spite of the limitations of hand spinning and the restricted range of vegetable dye substances, the ingenuity of these early workers enabled them to produce cloths which it would be hard to beat today, in spite of all our modern resources.

As early as the 9th century we have at Trinity College in Dublin the books of Kells and Durrow, whose authors lavished on them the most loving care in the illustrations, which are photographic in their fine detail, and from these we can even see the patterns which were woven into the cloth from which the vestments were made; from the way in which the garments fall into graceful folds we can infer that the cloth must have been both fine and soft in texture and rich in ornament.

In the Middle Ages began the production of tapestries which were not only masterpieces in their own right, but were highly pictorial in design. From these we are able to see that not only were sacred and royal persons gorgeously arrayed but the crowds of common people with whom the designers loved to fill their pictures were dressed in fabrics of great and varied beauty.

One of the most interesting of these tapestries is still preserved in the magnificent Guild Hall built at Coventry in the 15th century by the members of the Guilds of St. John, St. Katherine and the Trinity, and known as St. Mary's Hall. During the Wars of the Roses the city was intensely loyal to the Lancastrian cause and King Henry VI and his queen Margaret were frequent visitors. As an expression of loyalty some unknown benefactor gave a magnificent tapestry which fills the whole end wall of the great hall. In it are portrayed among figures of saints and angels many of the leading political persons of the period. From a study of these we get a vivid picture of the richness and variety of the clothes of the period.

Finally, we have the evidence of the early painters who depicted in great detail the clothes of their characters. A visit to any art gallery which has a collection of 14th- and 15th-century paintings will furnish abundant evidence of the richness and variety of the fabrics characteristic of the period.

All the evidence therefore shows Coventry as a medieval city of great wealth and prosperity created and sustained by the skill of its craftsmen and framed in a system of local government showing a high degree of social consciousness. And one would expect it to have developed and expanded with the growth in population and prosperity of the nation; yet within 200 years it had shrunk to a miserable remnant of its former greatness.

Many causes worked to bring this about, most of them being social, political and economic, and they are outside the scope of this book; but one is different and worthy of study, because it illustrates how, because of his inherent qualities, the craftsman is destined to feel the wind of change. Because his life is a struggle against the reluctance of material to accept the form he wishes to impose upon it, he is equally interested both in ends and means; and by means we imply the tools and machinery employed; and this brings into play man's inventive faculty.

To the Victorians this seemed not only a splendid thing in itself but entirely beneficial in its effects. This was because those effects which were pleasant, such as an increase of prosperity, were felt at home, while those which were painful were suffered by foreigners. The mechanisation of weaving and spinning and the developments in iron and steel may have made Lancashire and Sheffield rich, but they had a devastating effect on the native industries of other countries whose economies rested on more primitive techniques.

Today we are all too familiar with the problems arising from the growth of oil at the expense of coal, and of the internal combustion engine at that of steam power; but it is surprising to discover in the 14th century a technological revolution which drove the wool weaving industry away from cities such as Coventry and encouraged it in rural areas along the flanks of the Pennines and even as far as the Lake District.

This development was the invention of the power-driven fulling mill, which called for an abundant supply of fast flowing water, something which Coventry's local brook, the Sherbourne, could not possibly supply. The traditional method of compacting and finishing cloth was by coating it with soap and fuller's earth, and then laboriously tramping it under foot; this explains why the guild controlling this industry was known as Fullers and Walkers.

As soon as it was discovered that by mounting cams on a shaft turned by a water wheel, it was possible to operate wooden hammers or beetles under which the cloth could be drawn forward with little effort, the old laborious method was doomed. As the mountain uplands which furnished the water power were also ideal for the grazing of sheep, the centre of gravity of the weaving industry moved steadily northward; a process which was hastened by the behaviour of the guildsmen who with rising prosperity had tended to become more and more monopolistic in their behaviour. An abundance of cheap labour and an absence of restrictive practices could only have one outcome. In the case of Leicester it was said that there remained but one fuller in the town and 'He a poor man'.

Fortunately for Coventry a new industry, also textile, was growing up, the making of woollen caps and felt hats, which became so famous that a flourishing export trade to the Continent developed. The city Leet book shows that so important did this become that in 1496 the authorities granted guild status to the Cappers; a company which still survives although its functions are now purely social. Among the ruins of the Cathedral, which was destroyed in the war, is the Capper's Chapel, now restored and in regular use. A regulation made in the 14th century ordered that on Sundays the master men 'Each with his apprentices before him' should go to church. Churchmanship and craftsmanship were intimately linked together and we find theologians, such as St. Thomas Aquinas, devoting a good deal of attention to such problems as just prices and fair wages and expressing strong views on the offences of 'Forestalling, engrossing and regrating', devices which we today should call profiteering and rather mildly deplore as being 'against the public interest'; they more robustly spoke of them as abominations and iniquities.

Changes of fashion gradually destroyed the capper's trade, even though in an attempt to encourage it a regulation was passed making it obligatory for caps to be worn on holy days.

So by the end of Elizabeth's reign the trade of the city had once more declined, but a new chapter was about to unfold and for the next 250 years the name of Coventry was to become famous all over the world for a specialised product—ribbon—which by 1818 gave employment to 10,000 people and in 1857 to 25,000.

In 1627 the Leet book records the formation of a Silkweaver's Company, but records are scanty and it was not till the end of the century that, following the revocation of the Edict of Nantes,

Huguenot refugees came to the city, bringing with them a new art already highly developed in the area of France round about St. Etienne. Essentially a domestic industry, ribbon weaving was the foundation of great prosperity in which the role of the independent craftsman weaver was all-important. Not till very late in the story did factories, as we know them today, become common and even when they did it was normal for a manufacturer to produce only part of his output on his factory looms; what were known as 'outdoor weavers' survived in diminishing numbers right up to the 1914 war.

While other cities such as Birmingham, Manchester and Sheffield were following the well-known lines of development characteristic of the Industrial Revolution, Coventry pursued its own course, preserving many of the features it had acquired in the 17th century. How it was able to resist the powerful forces of change for so long and the ultimate consequences of this arrested growth, makes an interesting chapter of economic history.

First of all we must look at the physical features of the city to which the Huguenots brought the new industry of ribbon weaving. Nearly two miles long, measured on its major axis, it was only about half a mile wide so that open fields were never far from the busy streets, and these fields were the Lammas and Michaelmas lands owned and rigidly controlled by the freemen. Therefore the physical size of the city was fixed because no building land was available and so as this industry, together with the city's other trade, watchmaking, flourished, an intense pressure built up. We today are familiar with the fact that a Victorian house with a large garden may be worth more for its site value than as property; but that is exactly what happened in Coventry two centuries ago. When the Industrial Revolution was in full flood and cities such as Birmingham were developing factories on available land, Coventry was unable to follow this trend; but the large gardens of the Georgian houses were suitable for development as courts. In the lower floors the families lived while in the top weaving or watchmaking could be carried on. Thus the nature of the trade and the environment worked together to produce the conditions which finally caused a sad end to the story.

The organisation of the industry was quite different from that of the medieval cloth trade in which the weaver craftsman was also a trader. Whereas in the ribbon industry two separate classes of person had grown up—the weaver who owned the looms and sold his skilled services to the manufacturer who bought the raw material, usually silk, organised the primary processes of dyeing, winding and warping, and finally, after the goods were woven, was responsible for selling them. Thus the fixed capital invested in property and machinery was furnished by the weavers as well as the labour; while the liquid capital, mainly stock-in-trade, was found by the manufacturers.

George Eliot's 'Middlemarch' is really Coventry and the book gives an accurate picture of the times, based on personal observation by the author who had many friends in the city.

Two types of loom were employed, the simple hand loom producing only one ribbon at a time, although that could be of the greatest complexity; and the Dutch Engine Loom, an early attempt at automation. Because in ribbon weaving the warps are narrow it was possible to mount several of them side by side and to provide each one with a separate shuttle, but to have all the shuttles and the shedding mechanism operated from a master crank. This gave a much greater output per worker, but as its use was limited to very narrow and technically simple patterns the two types continued to exist side by side.

Steam power came into the story at a relatively late date. Records show that in the 1830's, an unfortunate, even if progressive, Mr. Beck not only had his looms burnt but he himself was tied backwards on a donkey and ignominiously paraded through the streets.

The life of the independent Coventry weaver was reasonably prosperous when compared with that of workers in other cities, and because they worked at home the men were able to regulate their hours of work to suit their own convenience and this usually meant not working on a Monday.

A sidelight is thrown on the prosperity of the Coventry weavers by a story which comes from the local press where we learn that they, being in high spirits and contemptuous of their fellow watchmakers who were having a slump, inserted an advertisement saying:

Wanted—Twenty poor watchmakers to shell peas for the weavers

The riot which followed had to be put down by the police.

This aggressive side of the weavers' character was not only shown in Coventry. In 1664 Pepys records in his diary that there was 'Great discoarse of the fray yesterday in Moorfields, how the butchers did at first beat the weavers (between whom there hath been ever an old competition for mastery) but at last the weavers rallied and beat them. At first the butchers knocked down all for weavers that had green or blue aprons, till they were fain to pull them off and put them in their breeches. At last the butchers were fain to pull of their sleeves that they might not be known, and were soundly beaten out of the field, and some deeply wounded and bruised, till at last the weavers went out triumphing, calling One Hundred Pounds for a butcher."

When in the 1850's there began the building of factories of the type we know today, there was strong opposition from the old weavers who resented bitterly the loss of independence as well as economic freedom. The result was a curious development, peculiar to Coventry, whereby independence and steam power could be enjoyed simultaneously; this was the cottage factory which consisted of a row of cottages each having a top weaving shop through which ran a common driving shaft coupled to a steam engine. Thus the landlord provided accommodation and power, and the weaver retained his independent status. The ingenious Mr. Eli Green developed a triangular site in Hillfields where, by some masterpiece of mill gearing, three rows of weaving shops were supplied with power from a centrally placed engine. The writer's grandfather rented one of these properties in Vernon Street and had his looms there for many years.

Old pattern books of the ribbon produced as far back as 1845 are in existence. What impresses one most strongly about them is the immense variety of skill and ingenuity possessed by these

weavers, who, it must be remembered, were their own maintenance mechanics and were responsible not only for running but also
for setting up the looms.

But the end of the story was inevitable—in 1860 the government negotiated a free-trade treaty with France under which
foreign competition became intense so that the last forty years of
the 19th century were a period of decline. Those manufacturers
who had gone in for modern industrial systems survived; but the
craft weaver, partly because he was part of an economically
unsound system and also because he lacked the financial resources
to enable him to adopt new and advanced techniques, gradually
faded out of the picture. This does not mean to say that craftsmanship disappeared, but after 1860 it became part of the modern
industrial system.

The last chapter of the textile history of Coventry has an ironic
twist which Hardy might have appreciated. The medieval
craftsmen who were also agriculturalists created the common
lands, which gave rise to the peculiar economic situation which,
during the late 18th and early 19th centuries, insulated Coventry
from the main stream of the Industrial Revolution, and so kept
alive a domestic system that can only be described as an anach-
ronism. Between about 1860 and 1870 therefore two things
happened at once, although from different causes. The freemen's
restrictive hold over the Lammas and Michaelmas Lands was
broken and the ribbon trade, on which the prosperity of the city
had for so long rested, declined. So at the very moment when
contraction rather than expansion became the operative factor
there suddenly became available a good deal of land ripe for
industrial development.

With land and labour available, Coventry became a desirable
home for the newer industries which were developing in the last
years of the 19th century. Bicycles, leading later to motor cars
and aircraft, were one part of the new age which was dawning,
but among those who were persuaded to select Coventry as a home
for a new invention were Messrs. Courtaulds who in 1905 set up
their first Rayon plant. Hence today among the young men and
women who seek admission to the freedom of the city are a

considerable number trained by this firm. Chemistry, physics and engineering may have replaced manual dexterity but the tradition of textile craftsmanship goes on.

The story of what happened in Coventry was broadly true of other centres such as Spitalfields in London, Derby, Macclesfield and Leek. The domestic system passed away leaving Lancashire and Yorkshire as the dominant textile areas.

The old industrial system may have passed away but the craftsman lives on and is still marked by a strong devotion to the maintenance of standards and the promotion of his art. When the old guilds broke up, some of their functions, which were mercantile, passed over to trade associations nation-wide in scope or to trade unions which were economic and political in outlook; but there were still in existence men whose first love was the mystery of their craft and it was the drawing together of these men which led to the foundation of two societies that today play an active part in modern life—The Textile Institute and The Shirley Institute, or to give the latter its full official title 'The Cotton, Silk and Man-made Fibres Research Association'.

Officially these are quite independent bodies but as they have many members in common and pursue, by slightly different paths, the same ends we can treat them as two aspects of the same thing. Behind each of them is the same driving force, a sincere belief that textile technology is an academic discipline and therefore the object of disinterested devotion and a worthy objective in the search for truth.

If Edward III was in some degree the father of the Guilds it was to King Charles II that we owe a debt of gratitude for the part he played in the story of pure and applied science. Professional historians scarcely bother to record that this brilliant man found pleasure in attending the meetings of the Royal Society and by taking part in discussions and debates gave encouragement and patronage to the scientific revolution, which was so soon to change the whole pattern of national life and among other things was to change the old craftsman into the modern technologist.

Out of these activities grew the learned societies or institutes, each promoting some special aspect of learning. Royal charters

K

endowed them with legal authority to govern themselves and to regulate the admission of candidates for membership. Only to persons found to be worthy both in character and learning was the door opened to the coveted distinction of fellowship.

The Textile Institute was one of these bodies and is empowered by Royal Charter to function as a degree awarding body and to act in any way desirable for the encouragement and promotion of textile technology.

Unlike Universities and Colleges, which usually regard the granting of a degree or certificate as the end of a story, the Textile Institute sees this only as a beginning and so post-graduate work is its main preoccupation. By organising conferences and lectures, and especially by the publication of journals, it forms a valuable channel through which its members are intellectually nourished while at the same time they provide the means whereby research workers can secure world-wide publicity for their ideas.

Disputation being the breath of life to scholars, it is by the organisation of conferences that the Institute carries out its main work. In addition to the great annual conference there are strong local centres scattered all over the world. Manchester, Hong Kong, Ahmedabad, Dublin and Pretoria are only a few of the places where technologists meet for exchanging information and to maintain the corporate life which means so much to them.

Specialist groups also meet for the exchange of knowledge on subjects as diverse as Physics and Industrial Archeology or for the drawing up and publishing of Textile Terms and Definitions.

Quality Control is a subject which appears again and again at conferences or in published papers and forms a link with the old guildsmen who never ceased to wage war on those who by carelessness or by deliberate malpractice injured the reputation of their craft. We read that, as far back as 1588: 'Certain evil-disposed persons, who buy and engross great store of linen cloth, do cast the pieces of cloth over a beam or piece of timber made for their purpose, and do by sundry devices rack, stretch, and draw the same both of length and breadth, and that done do then with battledores, pieces of timber and wood, and other things sore beat the same, even casting thereupon certain deceitful liquors mingled with chalk and other things, whereby the said cloth is not only made to seem much thicker and finer to the eye than it is indeed but also the thread thereof being so loosed and made weak, that after three or four washings it will hardly hold together, to the great loss and hindrance of the natives.' These practices were forbidden. Today the fight for quality is carried on by the British Standards Institute on whose committees the members of the Textile Institute play an active part.

Unnoticed by the outside world the Textile Institute has played a major part in a revolution which has gone on during the last fifty years; textile craftsmanship has changed from a traditional art based on empirical methods to a branch of applied science, a subject to which the older universities paid scant attention; but one to which the newer ones have given recognition by making it a degree subject. Leeds and Manchester and the University of New South Wales are among those who award the degree of Hons. B.Sc. in textile technology, engineering, colour chemistry or B.A. in textile design. In the New University of Warwick a further step has been taken by the recognition of Technology in general as an academic discipline in its own right.

The change from the empirical to the scientific outlook could not have taken place but for the establishment of research institutes; because it is not enough to know how things are done; if progress is to be made we must know why. Traditional skill breaks down when faced with new materials and processes. It was the recognition of this truth that led to the formation of research centres such as Lambeg for linen, Torredon for wool or Shirley for Cotton, Silk and Man-Made fibres.

Because they must pursue a threefold activity, these bodies are organised in a special way differentiating them from those where pure scientific research is carried on. Intimately linked there must be first the exploration of fundamental principles so that the frontiers of knowledge can be advanced; secondly, the critical examination of established techniques; and thirdly, because the final object of the work must be the practical application of knowledge, resources for carrying out large-scale tests that reproduce conditions which will be found in industry. So we find that in parallel with the laboratories where pure scientific research is carried on, there are complete installations of machinery on which large-scale tests can be made. Just as in aerodynamics the work of the theorist must be tested out in the wind tunnel, so in textiles the abstract and the practical must go hand-in-hand. Intellectual ivory towers form no part of the architecture in these research centres. Their windows are always wide open to the outside world of scientific progress. Computers, radio-active isotopes, electronic devices and electron microscopes are among the tools now being used for textile research.

All this activity, financed by contributions from industry and grants from government funds, is matched by the private research carried out by the great fibre producers such as Courtaulds and I.C.I. whose laboratories cover many acres and employ hundreds of scientists and technicians.

So the story of the textile craftsman unfolds as part of man's struggle to improve and progress; neolithic men solved the basic problems of spinning and weaving; Kaye, Cartwright and Crompton changed laborious hand methods to automatic machine ones; Chardonnet and Bevan blazed the trail which led to the replacement of natural by synthetic fibres; Perkin showed how from coal tar or petroleum a richer palette of colours could be evolved; and today the research worker pushes forward the frontiers of knowledge; all are united by one common bond, the incurable itch to expand and improve the most beautiful of all the useful arts.

Glossary of Technical Terms

Alpaca. The silky fleece of a South American animal like a llama inhabiting the Andes at 14,000–16,000 feet. Also the name of a fine cloth made from the yarn.

Angora. Yarn spun from goat hair.

Axminster. A form of carpet in which normal warp and weft form a canvas foundation into which decorative pile is inserted by spools.

Barathea. Strictly a very fine basket weave which can be made from any material. Commonly used to describe a fine worsted cloth.

Batten. The reciprocating part of the loom which carries the reed or slay and the shuttle mechanism.

Batik. An ancient Javanese form of fabric pattern dyeing. Those parts of the fabric not to be coloured are protected by a coating of wax.

Beam. The roll supplying warp to the loom.

Beating up. The driving home of a pick of weft by the reed or slay, so that it lies parallel and as close as possible to its neighbours.

Beetling. From 'beetle', a heavy wooden mallet. In cloth finishing the compacting of the warp and weft by beating.

Blanket. Woollen fabric brushed after weaving to produce pile.

Bonchon. 1725, the inventor of punched cards, later incorporated by Jacquard.

Brocade. Ornamental figure work superimposed on a plain weave by free floating weft threads.

Carding. The brushing of fibres with a steel wire brush in order to lay them parallel and to remove trash.

Chenille. French for hairy caterpillar. Yarn made by cutting fabric into very narrow strips from the edges of which the severed weft threads protrude like bristles. Also used to describe cloth woven from such material.

Celanese. The proprietary name for rayon spun from cellulose *acetate.*

Cockling. Local distortion of the surface of a cloth owing to differences in shrinkage of yarns.

Combing. The selection of long from short fibres to improve quality of yarn.

Cotton. The fibrous protective coat surrounding the seed pod of the cotton bush.

Couching. The application of thick threads, often of metal wire, to the surface of embroidery by using extremely fine tacking stitches.

Coventry Blue. Old manuscripts often use the phrase 'True as Coventry Blue', but nobody knows the precise colour—the adjective 'true' probably refers to fastness.

Crêpe. A generic term for fabrics made from highly twisted yarns which contort owing to the strain and so give the fabric a moss effect.

Cross. The arrangement of warp threads by passing them alternately over and under two pegs so that they are kept in perfect sequent order.

Damask. Figured cloth made by combining satin weave woven face up or face down so giving a two-tone effect. Name derived from Damascus where this fabric was said to have originated.

Denier. A small unit of weight used in France before the metric system was introduced. Now used as unit for expressing the size of silk and other filament yarns. Internationally defined as the weight in grams of 9,000 metres.

Double Cloth. A fabric woven with two warps bound by a common weft. Often used for men's overcoats, the one warp forming a tweed while the other makes a patterned lining.

Dobby. Automatic shedding mechanism used on power looms. Working on the Jacquard principle it lifts the shafts in plain looms. Its pattern making scope is limited as it usually has twenty-four or less hooks.

Drafting. (A) The attenuating of fibre yarns to increase their fineness prior to spinning. (B) The setting out of a design on squared paper in Jacquard weaving.

Draw Loom. The forerunner of the Jacquard. The selection of the threads to form a pattern was done by plucking cords.

Drop Box. A small frame with horizontal slots, each carrying a shuttle of a different colour. By raising and lowering the box any desired shuttle can be brought into the operating position.

Dutch Engine. Invented early in the 17th century. A multi-shuttle loom by means of which a number of ribbons could be woven simultaneously.

Embroidery. Decoration applied by means of a needle to a previously woven cloth.

Faller. A wire having an eyelet in its tip through which thread passes when being spun. By a change in the position of the wire the two operations of spinning are regulated, in twisting and winding up.

Folded Yarns. Two or more strands are twisted together to form a cable which is stronger and more uniform than the equivalent single thread.

Fell. The exact point to which the reed drives the weft, sometimes used to describe the short length of cloth exposed near the breast rail of the loom.

Felt. A non-woven fabric made by beating wool fibres whose natural cohesion forms a solid mass.

Fly Shuttle. Invented by John Kay, 1733. A means of propelling the shuttle by sliding blocks, which are jerked by a cord, thus enabling the weaver to have one hand free for other tasks.

Fustian. Widely used in Middle Ages. A cloth woven with loops of weft which were afterwards cut with a fine pointed knife to form a pile.

Galloon. Fine corded ribbon with a characteristic bead edge. Commonly used on men's felt or bowler hats.

Gin. The machine used by cotton growers to separate by spiked rollers the fibres from the cotton seeds.

Griffe. Part of the Jacquard machine, consisting of a rectangular frame carrying knife-edge bars with which the selected hooks engage and are so lifted.

Grogram. From the French 'Grosgrain', a heavy corded weave. An 18th-century British admiral had a cloak of this cloth, his nickname was 'Old Grog' and he was the originator of the issue of rum to the navy, hence the name 'Grog' for a mixture of rum and water.

Headles. See shafts.

Jacquard. Selector mechanism working on the punched card principle; used in figure looms for making elaborate patterns. Named after the inventor Joseph Marie Jacquard, born Lyons 1752.

Leish. The control thread bearing an eyelet through which a warp thread passes and is thereby caused to rise or fall and so make a shed.

Linen. Yarn spun from the strong fibres of the flax plant.

Lingo. A thin length of wire attached to each leish of a Jacquard harness, causing it to fall when the griffe is lowered.

Moiré. A water wave surface pattern formed on corded fabrics by heat and pressure which flatten the ribs and so alters their light reflecting properties.

Nylon. The first truly man-made fibre—not found in nature, it is a complex molecule built up from simple elements.

Opus Anglicanum. A medieval term for the English school of ecclesiastical embroidery.

Organzine. Real silk highly twisted to give extra strength for use as warp.

Pick. (*a*) One revolution of the crank shaft of a loom causing one passage of a shuttle across the warp.
(*b*) A thread of weft from selvedge to selvedge.

Pirn. A slender, taper-ended bobbin carrying the weft yarn in the shuttle.

Porry. The stretched portion of the warp behind the harness of the loom.

Quill. A small bobbin carrying weft in a shuttle. Synonymous with 'Pirn', but mostly used in the ribbon trade.

Rayon. The generic term for man-made fibres made from regenerated cellulose. Usually sold under proprietary names such as Viscose, Bemberg, Celanese, etc.

Reed. A fine comb mounted on the batten of the loom. Its two functions are to distribute the warp ends evenly across the fabric and to beat up the weft after the shuttle has laid it across the warp.

Resist. A protective layer of insoluble gum or varnish used to protect selected areas of cloth from the action of dye liquor.

Retting. The process of soaking flax in water and leaving it to ferment so as to separate out the linen fibres.

Roving. Fibres laid parallel and slightly twisted ready for spinning. The accuracy with which the roving is drawn out governs size and uniformity.

Satin. A weave having long warp floats which give high lustre. Not a fibre or raw material.

Screen Printing. A process of decorating fabric by a form of stencil made by blocking up desired parts of a fine silk gauze leaving other parts open for the penetration of a dye paste.

Serge. Wool cloth, first woven in Spain as blanket called Xerga.

Shaft. Thin slats of wood supporting the leishes by which the warp threads are controlled in plain looms.

Shed. The V-shaped opening formed by the warp for the passing of the shuttle.

Shedding. The separation of the threads of the final product of a warp into layers between which the shuttle, by its passage, lays a weft thread.

Shoddy. Yarn spun from shredded wool rags.

Shot Silk. A fine taffeta woven with contrasting colours of warp and weft.

Shuttle. A boat-shaped object which is propelled from side to side in the loom, carrying with it the weft.

Silk. The thread which forms the cocoon of the silkworm (usually *Bombyx mori*). The use of this term as a description of any other yarn is an offence under the Merchandise Marks Act.

Simple. The control cords by which the loom harness was operated in the draw loom.

Slay. Synonymous with Reed, q.v.

Sliver. Fibres which have been combed or carded into parallel order but not yet spun into thread.

Stenter. A cloth finishing machine in which the fabric is kept under tension while drying by exposure to hot air.

Tapestry. Decorative, usually pictorial, fabric formed by interweaving thick weft on a plain warp, the fabric and the pattern being formed in one operation.

Tappet. A lever depressed by a cam in the shedding mechanism.

Tatting. The making of ornamental net work, similar to crochet; but done with a shuttle instead of a hook.

Temples. Rollers with spirally arranged teeth like those of a nutmeg grater. Fitted at the selvedges they serve to stretch the cloth to full width.

Tentering. The stretching of cloth to full width by means of endless chains carrying sharp hooks. Having gripped the cloth the chains move apart and so exert tension. Hence the expression 'On tenterhooks'.

Throwing. The process of imparting twist to continuous filament yarns. The operative is known as a Throwster.

Thrum. The waste end of a warp, too short to weave.

Topping. A malpractice in dyeing whereby a fugitive tint is added to produce an effect of brilliance not otherwise obtainable.

Tjanting. A small metal pot having a very fine spout, used for applying molten wax to fabric which is to be dyed by the batik process.

Tussah or Tussore. Natural silk obtained from the cocoons of wild silkworms found in India and Assam. The impurities in the leaves on which the worms feed give this silk a pale brownish tint.

Tweed. Literally twilled cloth or tweels. A London merchant Mr. Locke (1831) misread the word and in error ordered tweeds, and so a mistake gave a new word to the dictionary.

Twill. A fabric having a pronounced diagonal trail.

Vat. The tank with which the dyer works. Also a type of dye liquor chemically reduced to a form capable of being absorbed by fibres and subsequently fixed by oxidation to form a durable pigment firmly bound inside the fibres.

Viscose. Noun = The glutinous fluid form of cellulose xanthate from which threads are spun by extrusion. Adjective = Rayon made by this process.

Warp. Strong threads running from end to end of a fabric. The foundation of all fabrics.

Weft. The thread carried by the shuttle and laid from selvedge to selvedge. Usually of soft yarn.

Wilton. High quality carpet in which a warp and weft form the canvas back which is ornamented by pile formed from extra warps.

Woof. A word never used by weavers to whom it is meaningless. A 'precious' word used by authors, poets and clergy.

Worsted. Strictly a process whereby long staple wool is spun into fine strong yarn for suitings. It is not a material although it is used to describe the cloth for which it is chiefly used.

BIBLIOGRAPHY

MILDRED J. DAVIS: *The Art of Crewel Embroidery*. Studio Vista, 1962.

N. KREVITSKY: *Batik Art and Craft*. Reinhold Publishing Corporation.

JANET ERICKSON: *Block Printing on Textiles*. Watson Guptill, New York.

VICTOR W. VON HAGEN: *The Desert Kingdoms of Peru*. Weidenfeld & Nicolson, 1965. Deals with pre-Inca civilisation and has a well illustrated section on textiles.

CHAMBERS' ENCYCLOPAEDIA: *See Carpets, Rugs, Woven Fabrics*.

AJIT MOOKERJEE: *Designs in Indian Textiles*. The Indian Institute of Art in Industry, Artistry House, Park Street, Calcutta.

ENCYCLOPAEDIA BRITANNICA: see Tapestry: a history of this art with copious illustrations, some in colour; Carpets; Weaving.

STEPHEN RUSS: *Fabric Printing by Hand*. Studio Vista, 1964.

J. H. STRONG: *Foundations of Fabric Structure*. National Trade Press, 1946. An excellent textbook, well illustrated.

Gospel Stories in English Embroidery. Victoria and Albert Museum.

HARRIETTE J. BROWN: *Hand-Weaving for Pleasure and Profit*. Faber and Faber, 1954.

A. BARLOW: *The History and Principles of Weaving*, 1878.

C. DELABÈRE MAY: *How to Identify Persian Rugs*. G. Bell and Sons, Ltd., 1952.

HEINRICH JACOBY: *How to Know Oriental Carpets and Rugs*. Allen and Unwin, 1953.

SONIA COLE: *The Neolithic Revolution*. British Museum. H.M. Stationers Office, 1959. Very well illustrated. Gives a clear account of Neolithic man's ingenuity in many fields, as well as in textiles.

Notes on Carpet Knotting and Weaving. Victoria and Albert Museum, H.M. Stationers Office, 1920. A simple and clear account of the various techniques used in oriental textiles. It has a simple diagram from which anyone interested could build a hand loom for experimenting in tapestry or pile weaving.

PREBEN LIEBETRAU: *Oriental Rugs in Colour*. Collier-Macmillan, 1963.

AVERIL COLBY: *Samplers: Yesterday and Today*. B. T. Batsford, 1964.

MARY MEIGS ATWATER: *The Shuttle-craft Book of American Hand-weaving*. The Macmillan Company, 1947. A full account of the hand-loom weaving practised in the U.S.A. by early settlers. Fully illustrated and provided with technical data taken from old weavers' notebooks.

The Silk Book. Silk and Rayon Users' Association, 1951. Although this deals with a single fibre, it describes, in simple language, all the basic textile processes.

BARBARA MORRIS: *Victorian Embroidery*. Herbert Jenkins, 1962.

L. E. SIMPSON and M. WEIR: *The Weaver's Craft*. Dryad Press, 1932.

Index